When God Is Not Finished With You Yet

When God Is Not Finished With You Yet

BISHOP DR. MERCY WOOD

DIP.MT; DM

WOOD WORLD MISSIONS

238-240 London Road
Mitcham
Surrey,
CR4 3HD
United Kingdom

Copyright © 2020 by Bishop Dr. Mercy Wood

The right of *Bishop Dr. Mercy Wood* to be identified as the author of this work has been asserted by him in accordance with the Copyright, Designs and Patents Act 1988.

All rights reserved.
Without limiting the rights under copyright above, no part of this publication shall be reproduced, stored in or introduced into a retrieval system, or transmitted in any form or by any means (electronic, mechanical, photocopying, recording or otherwise), without the prior permission of the copyright owner.

ISBN: 9798661210982 (paperback edition)

KJV – Authorised version of the Bible. *All Bible quotations are used by permission.*

Printed in England

DEDICATION

I would like to dedicate this revised edition to the memory of my late dad—Mr. Isaac KariKari and my late mother-in-law—Madam Elizabeth Davidson, for all the support they gave me when they were alive. May their souls continue to rest in perfect peace.

TABLE OF CONTENTS

I. Author's Note 1

1. When God is Not Finished With You 3

2. When You Feel Like Giving Up 9

3. How the Missions Came About 17

4. Tanzania Mission 21

5. The Goma And Uganda Mission 26

6. Ethiopian Mission Experience 75

7. What Inspires Me to Do What I Do 92

8. Malawi Mission Experience 111

AUTHOR'S NOTE

I would like to thank the Almighty God for giving me an insight into His word concerning our Lord and Saviour Jesus Christ. Thank you, Lord, for protecting us and providing for us on our mission trips.

I would like to thank my husband Bishop Dr. William Wood. You have been my pillar of support, strength and encouragement. Thank you for taking the time to read through this book before I sent it off to the publishers. To our wonderful son Gabriel Wood, thank you for being a wonderful and obedient son. Thanks to my nephews Kobi Mintah, Prince, and all Team Salute members.

Thank you Brother Ivor Patnelli for taking the time to proofread this book in its initial stage. To all our partners around the world who have supported our ministry, I say God bless you.

To Apostle Janet Karikari and all members of Power Centre Church, thank you for your constant support to the charity. {Brown Envelopes}

I do appreciate Oasis church elders and members who were a great blessing to us by paying for our shipping costs and supporting us to accomplish the work of God in the early days of our *Ministry*. May the Lord bless you.

I am indebted to Dorothy Lock, Bob and Dorothy Cromwell for supporting us in every way they could—and to Lady Roberta Atkinson, Chris Hpa, Pastor James Mwesigwa and Pastor Charles Wilson for accompanying me on my Goma trip.

To all members of *Power Centre Church*, Pastors, Elders & Deacons, Deaconesses and to all our Minister Friends—God richly bless you for your perpetual support. Your labour in the Lord shall never be in vain.

—Bishop Dr. Mercy Wood

Dip.MT. DM

Director of Mission Projects

Wood World Missions

Chapter 1
WHEN GOD IS NOT FINISHED WITH YOU YET

Pursuing Your God-given assignment

When God says your time is not due yet, it is because He has an assignment for you to do on earth. God calls people to do His work here on earth with different assignments and purposes. God can use anybody, anytime, anywhere. God can do anything in His time. God can choose any of us. It is up to us to accept or deny His call. Up to us to say *"Yes, Lord send me, and I will go,"* or dodge Him just as Jonah did which ended him in the belly of a Whale. I suppose you remember the story: Jonah thought he could run away from God. God sent the whale to remind us all that none of us can run away from Him; that He is omnipotent, omnipresent, omniscient. We should be wise and rather heed to His call. Because the world has nothing for us. Everything we want is in Christ Jesus. Let's not harden our hearts.

Jesus said in John 15:16, *"You did not choose Me, but I chose you. I appointed you that you should go out and produce fruit and that your fruit should remain, so that whatever you ask the Father in My name, He will give you."*

Jesus also said to His disciples, *"If anyone wants to come with Me, he must deny himself, take up his cross, and follow Me."*

Doing the will of the Father can take you through issues, pains, sacrifices even betrayals from people closer to you. But if God Himself called you, He will see you through.

A lot of people find my story so unique. They ask me all the time, "Why are you so committed to charitable works? Because of this work, you nearly died. You ended up breaking your pelvis and your hand. What's so distinctive about *charity works* that fuels you, that keeps you going?

Well, the only answer I have for them is God. I say God because this is the assignment, He has given me. And just as teachers do get disappointed when students fail to do their homework, I do not want to disappoint my Father in Heaven when the time comes for me to stand before Him and give an account of what I did with my life. I want to let Him know that even though it took me a while, I still did His work. This is what God has embedded in me to do on this earth. This is why I am here, why I am breathing, why I will continue to. And without the guidance and constant support of my husband, Bishop Dr. William Wood, it would have been extremely difficult. Even with both of us working together for the Lord, we do have our difficulties, yet we continue to smile at the storm because God is in our vessel.

Here are some scriptures to help boost the immune system of your faith in God.

Philippians 1:6 says, *"Being confident of this very thing, that he which hath begun a good work in you will perform it until the day of Jesus Christ."*

We need to have a mind full of trust and assurance that surely our God will and can bring what He said to pass even in the midst of whatever you may be going through. When Joshua was discouraged because his mentor Moses was gone, God came in and encouraged him not to give up. Sometimes we go through situations which are not as a result of anything we have done wrong. Some circumstances can also generate doubts in our minds if we are not careful. In all these things, we need to have faith and hope in God.

Here was Joshua, who was working with his master whom he trusted so much. He learnt a lot from a hopeless situation when waiting on God on that mountain while Moses was talking to God. He saw what Moses did that gave him confidence. I want you to know that, *when your all seems lost, your all is never lost*. God is with you.

Joshua learnt a lot from Moses from their time in Egypt, through the Red sea experience, up to when Moses died.

Joshua 1:1-7 says: *"¹Now after the death of Moses the servant of the LORD it came to pass, that the LORD spake unto Joshua the son of Nun, Moses' minister, saying, ² Moses my servant is dead; now therefore arise, go over this Jordan, thou, and all these people, unto the land which I do give to them, even to the children of Israel. ³ Every place that the sole of your foot shall tread upon, that have I given unto you, as I said unto Moses. ⁴ From the wilderness and this Lebanon even unto the great river, the river Euphrates, all the land of the Hittites, and unto the great sea toward the going down of the sun, shall be your coast. ⁵ There shall not any man be able to stand before thee all the days of thy life: as I was with Moses, so I will be with thee: I will not fail thee, nor forsake thee. ⁶ Be strong and of a good courage: for unto this people shalt thou divide for an inheritance the land, which I sware unto their fathers to give them. ⁷ Only be thou strong and very courageous, that thou mayest observe to do according to all the law, which Moses my servant commanded thee: turn not from it to the right hand or to the left, that thou mayest prosper withersoever thou goest".*

God has many ways of elevating each one of us in His own time. All He expects of us is to trust and obey Him.

Psalm 46:1-3 says, *"God is our refuge and strength, an ever-present help in trouble. Therefore, we will not fear, though the earth give way and the mountains fall into the heart of the sea, though its waters roar and foam and the mountains quake with their surging".*

Psalm 145: 18-19 says *"The Lord is near to all who call on him, to all who call on him in truth. He fulfils the desires of those who fear him; he hears their cry and saves them. May the Lord hear your tears and answer you"?*

1 Peter 5:7 says, *"Casting all your care upon him; for he careth for you."*

Casting our cares and worries can sometimes be difficult owing to our own insecurities, which eventually leads us into trouble. That is why God says we should cast or bring that problem to Him so that He can sort it out for us. You don't need to carry it because it is too heavy of a load. Just allow God to carry it for you so that you can rest assured that all will be well. Your situation may be tough, but God can and will deliver you from it.

Isaiah 12:2 says *"Behold, God is my salvation; I will trust, and not be afraid: for the LORD JEHOVAH is my strength and my song; he has also become my salvation."*

God can do all things, sort out all things no matter what. Indeed, He is our Salvation.

Proverbs 18:10 says, *"The name of the LORD is a strong tower: the righteous runneth into it, and is safe."* He said

His hands are not short that He can't touch you, He is a safe place to hide when trouble comes".

Isaiah 41:10 *"Fear thou not; for I am with thee: be not dismayed; for I am thy God: I will strengthen thee; yea, I will help thee; yea, I will uphold thee with the right hand of my righteousness."*

Nehemiah 8: 10 says, *"Then he said unto them, Go your way, eat the fat, and drink the sweet, and send portions unto them for whom nothing is prepared: for this day is holy unto our Lord: neither be ye sorry; for the joy of the LORD is your strength."*

Exodus 15:2 also says, *"The LORD is my strength and song, and he has become my salvation: he is my God, and I will prepare Him an habitation; my father's God, and I will exalt him."*

The Lord is working on your behalf. Trust Him and He will deliver you. I have died, broken my pelvis, hip, my lips and my hand. This scripture helped me a lot.

Chapter 2
WHEN YOU FEEL LIKE GIVING UP

As a human being, there are days when you may feel the need to animate someone else's day, make life better for another person even when you are grappling with your own woes. In this interest, you may want to share what you have (*which is sometimes your all in all*) with others just as our Lord and Saviour Jesus Christ admonishes us to do. I must confess, though, that it is so sad when the very people you give your all to are mostly the very people that hurt you more. It is easy to throw in the towel when this happens. But you do not have to yield to such diplomacies of the enemy. You have to stay focused and keep carrying the cross. I do know that my assignment in this world is not to please anyone, so I am going to stay true to my God-given assignments and use my time and resources to create the most positive impact to as many people as I can. If people want to backstab, let them backstab, I will continue to pursue my God-given assignments. If they want to talk, as long as they are not using my mouth, they can go ahead. What people say does not matter as long as I am doing the will of my Father in Heaven. He is not a man to depend on people. Which is why I am encouraging you to stay focused because the good news is that God will never forsake you. He has a reward for your faithfulness. God appreciates you. He loves you. He appreciates your dedication.

The word of God assures us that Jesus will never leave nor forsake us. Sometimes when I see the needs of many pastors who have no one to help them, how they come asking for support, the thought of helping them is the last thing that comes to mind when I ruminate on those who betrayed us even after ordaining them.

We are always there for them—we help them with their home issues, we help them in every way possible, yet it is astounding to think of how unappreciative they are, how hasty they turn to give us a Judas kiss. Only God knows why such people do that. And so, obviously, this does not encourage us to help anyone else. But I take comfort in the fact that betrayals and backstabbing did not start today. Jesus felt the same way but because He is the Saviour, He encourages us through His word to persevere and be persistent in doing good. He encourages us not to give up in whatever we do. Giving up means you have failed. God has not called us to fail, He called us because He wants us to win. We are winners because of His blood He shed on the Cross of Calvary.

John 15:4 says *"Abide in me, and I in you. As the branch cannot bear fruit of itself, except it abides in the vine; no more can ye, except ye abide in me."*

All things are possible if you believe. Did you say if I believe? I am sure you are asking the same question: I have prayed and prayed but nothing has happened, why should I continue to believe? I say to you: pray again and again and again. Do not lose hope. Sometimes God answers so quickly, sometimes He seems to delay a bit but that does not mean He will not do it.

In my walk with God, my faith sometimes shakes a bit, too. Because I am human. When I need money to do a project, for example, and I am strapped for funds, all I do is speak to God. One of my conversations with Him is, *"Father, you know I urgently need this money for these orphans and school projects. This is not for my personal need. Please, speak to somebody somewhere to assist us."* And indeed, God never fails. He always comes through for us. Because with God all things are possible.

There are tons of examples of those who trusted God. With some of them, even though what they asked God for looked impossible, yet God answered them in the end. That reminds me of Queen Esther, the Orphan. God moved her from *'Nobody'* to *'Somebody'*. I want you to know that: the favour of God is at work. God is still in the business of favouring His children. Claim yours in Jesus' name.

Esther 2:15-17 says: *"Now when the turn of Esther, the daughter of Abihail the uncle of Mordecai, who had taken her for his daughter, was come to go in unto the king, she required nothing but what Hegai the king's chamberlain, the keeper of the women, appointed. And Esther obtained favour in the sight of all them that looked upon her. So, Esther was taken unto king Ahasuerus into his house royal in the tenth month, which is the month Tebeth, in the seventh year of his reign. And the king loved Esther above all the women, and she obtained grace and favour in his sight more than all the virgins; so that he set the royal crown upon her head, and made her queen instead of Vashti".*

That is what I call **FAVOUR**.

My childhood was an insufferable one. After my dear mother had passed away, I became an orphan, a hopeless girl. My future seemed so bleak. Making ends meet became my daily struggle. Nothing was promising about me if you saw me in my long, grimy dress in those days. With time, the presence of God became my place of solace. I started praying and seeking the face of God every blessed day.

As a young orphan, whenever I was in trouble, whenever I needed money for school fees, I talked to God in prayer. And amazingly, whenever I prayed to God about my situation, especially when it had to do with money, lo and behold, I would find money on the dirt streets.

My trust in God was and still is something I cannot even fathom. God loves me so much that whatever I ask Him for He answers me.

Like Queen Esther, God lifted me up from the miry place, from an orphan girl to become a Bishop, an Apostle, a Missionary, who is endlessly travelling to so many countries to preach the word of God and also helping to meet the needs of those who are in need. The struggles you are in today is developing the strength you need for tomorrow.

Do not let what you are going through discourage you. Let it excite you. Because when you are standing in the purity of the Word of God, you must know that everything is going to be all right.

If God can do this for me, He can do the same for you. If God is using me, He can use you if you avail yourself to Him.

Psalms 102:13 says, *"Thou shalt arise, and have mercy upon Zion: for the time to favour her, yea, the set time, is come."*

Yes, indeed, God is favouring me because my time has come. All these betrayals, pains, disappointments, you name it, that I encountered because of my passion to help people, surely God has seen it all. He will answer you because the Word of God says He will.

Ecclesiastes 9:11 says, *"I returned and saw under the sun, that the race is not to the swift, nor the battle to the strong, neither yet bread to the wise, nor yet riches to men of understanding, nor yet favour to men of skill; but time and chance happeneth to them all."*

Wow! I know God will surely answer us. We just need to believe and trust Him.

He said in Revelation 3:21 that *"To him that overcometh will I grant to sit with me in my throne, even as I also overcame, and am set down with my Father in his throne." If you have not gone through some issues and challenges, how can you say I am an overcomer.*

As I always say, "No Cross, No Crown".

Apostle Paul mentioned in Romans 8:24-39 that *"For we are saved by hope: but hope that is seen is not hope: for what a man seeth, why doth he yet hope for? But if we hope for that we see not, then do we with patience wait for it. Likewise, the Spirit also helpeth our infirmities: for we know not what we should pray for as we ought: but the Spirit itself maketh intercession for us with groanings which cannot be uttered. And he that searcheth the hearts knoweth what is the mind of the Spirit because he maketh intercession for the saints according to the will of God. And we know that all things work together for good to them that love God, to them who are called according to His purpose. For whom he did foreknow, he also did predestinate to be conformed to the image of his Son, that he might be the firstborn among many brethren. Moreover whom he did predestinate, them he also called: and whom he called, them he also justified: and whom he justified, them he also glorified.*

What shall we then say to these things? If God be for us, who can be against us? He that spared not his own Son, but delivered Him up for us all, how shall he not with him also freely give us all things? Who shall lay anything to the charge of God's elect? It is God that justifieth. Who is he that condemneth? It is Christ that died, yea rather, that is risen again, who is even at the right hand of God, who also maketh intercession for us. Who shall separate us from the love of Christ? shall tribulation, or distress, or persecution, or famine, or nakedness, or peril, or sword? As it is written, For thy sake we are killed all the day long; we are accounted as sheep for the slaughter.

Nay, in all these things we are more than conquerors through him that loved us. For I am persuaded, that neither death, nor life, nor angels, nor principalities, nor powers, nor things present, nor things to come, Nor height, nor depth, nor any other creature, shall be able to separate us from the love of God, which is in Christ Jesus our Lord".

This is to encourage us that nothing should stop us from serving our God.

When your bills are piling up; when you need to pay your child's school fees; when your job is not in good shape; when your marriage is in trouble; when your home is on fire; when your wife or your husband is nagging; when your child is sick and there is no money to take that child to the hospital; when there seems to be no hope, that is when you have to trust in the Lord and wait patiently for Him to come through for you. God sees the fruit of your struggles. Let go of yesterday's mistakes and focus on Him. When Christ died on the cross, redemption for each one of us became possible. All we have to do is to give our burdens to Him.

If your trust is in the Lord, you can confidently say that I know no matter what comes my way, NOTHING CAN STOP ME.

Chapter 3
HOW THE MISSIONS CAME ABOUT AND WHERE WE ARE NOW

It gives me great pleasure to share with you a bit about how the activities of the *Wood World Missions* began and, more importantly, where God is taking it.

In the first few years of our Ministry—on our trips to Ghana—we take with us clothes, books, stationery and several other items. On arrival, we would share them amongst the needy and less privileged, using the opportunity to preach the Word of God and win souls for our Lord Jesus Christ. We undertook these projects with our meagre resources. We have, over the years, helped to meet the needs of humanity in different parts of the world. We have had an impact on the spiritual, physical, emotional, psychological lives of many people.

Another thing that we came to realise was that when people received the gifts from us, it made them more receptive to the Word of God. With this in mind, we intensified our efforts in the year 2000 and we have never looked back since then.

We formally inaugurated the international section of the Wood World Missions on September 2nd, 2000. The inauguration, which was very well attended, had as its theme as *"A Time of Celebration."*

God has opened many doors for us to minister the Word as itinerary Ministers in the United Kingdom, United States of America, Ghana, Goma, Tanzania, Ethiopia, Malawi and many other places.

We have also helped to make many people's dreams come true. We have provided hospitals with beds and food. We have provided accommodation for the destitute, relief for the suffering. You name it—God has used us to bless and touch many people in many ways. It's such a humbling experience. We could not have done this without our faithful partners and friends. You rock!

I remember when I was first called into full-time ministry work around the world, I was a worker earning a stable income. Though it was not a huge salary, it kept us going. My dear husband was also working and studying to upgrade as a solicitor at the same time. God knows everything we do and think, because He created us.

When we began this charity mission work, we were using our own funds as I said before. Then God came in, asking me to give up my work and become a full-time Evangelist and Missionary. This meant I had to drop that job, that job which brought us some income to support the charity as well as our household. I sometimes get shocked how we were able to move our way through those turbulent years. Well, with God all things are possible, isn't it?

The first few months of ministry were satisfactory as I reminisce, but things ultimately started to dry up in the house. This convinced my husband to cut his pay to do his final training to qualify as a higher solicitor. For a whole year, our income was drastically reduced, but God moved in mysterious ways. The bills were paid, our boys were fed, the ministry was doing well—you name it. God provided without us having to receive any funds from the mission. I was not being paid but we decided to trust God.

During those days, our needs continued to be met daily. God is a wonderful provider. Amazingly, in the year 2002, I travelled to many countries more than ever. I remember calling some *Pastors*, *Evangelists*, *Financial Granters* and no one responded to our request to support our projects. It was devastating.

God then asked us to start planting a church. We did not hesitate; we only trusted His calling and began our first Church at Beddington Lane in Surrey England. Then He later asked us again to plant another in Clapham and Stockwell. Then churches began to spread like fire. Those in High Wycombe, in Malawi, in Ghana and in other countries—they were all growing well by the grace of God.

It has not been easy, but we are moving on. The rejection, the false promises. Some pastors did not want to have anything to do with us because they were frightened that we would pinch their members. How could we do? Praise be to God Almighty for showing Himself strong on our behalf.

Today my husband is a qualified Solicitor as well as a Minister of God, and we are helping many people with free legal advice referral service and counselling. Our God indeed is providing for all our needs.

We now have branches in the United Kingdom, High Wycombe, Manchester, Ghana, Nigeria, South Africa, Malawi, Zambia, Mozambique and other parts of the world. We have built schools in Malawi and in Ghana. We are also building a Youth Centre and a Church in Wakisa, Uganda. We are, with the help of our Mission Partners, currently building a Secondary, Technical and Vocational School in Akosombo, Ghana. We hope to complete it within the next 12 to 18 months. All glory be to our God.

We also have a Charity office in the USA. We thank the Lord for all that he is doing through us whilst we have life. All glory be to His name. Amen.

Chapter 4
TANZANIA MISSION

My Tanzania Experience

In December of the year 2000, while on a mission trip to Tanzania, I visited a Church school. This local church had been trying to help these children, but it was hard getting the materials they needed to assist in teaching the children. The headteacher asked if we could help them to improve the children's education. I found out that they had no proper tables and chairs for the children to write on. There was nothing for them to play with. There were no lights in the building, and the books were not enough for them to study. Shockingly, some of the children had never even seen a doll before.

The donations of our partners and well-wishers helped these children to progress with their education. Oasis Church children even collected some money for us to send to the school— pencils, pens, Bibles and children's books. After visiting the school, we went straight to the conference hall where thousands of people were seated and waiting for our appearance. The meeting was spiritually charged and electrifying, many people were touched by the awesome power and the presence of God through the Holy Spirit.

I spent ten days in this extraordinary conference, which was attended by many people from Zambia, Uganda, South Africa, and seventeen different rural areas of Tanzania, Kenya and other nearby countries.

God moved in many diverse ways. I was left speechless to hear that some people walked two to three days just to come to be a part of the conference. It was so wonderful to see people yearning for the Word of God, that they would undertake such an arduous journey to hear the Word of God. Here in the West you sometimes have to implore members and plead with them to come to church. Can you imagine asking them to walk or travel long distances to meetings? The women were happy and excited because they had not had a woman preacher for that year, as I was educated.

From that day, I was so blessed and challenged to do more for the Lord. There were aged women and men seated. One of them, an 85-year-old-woman, really touched my heart. She came to the meeting from a very long distance when she heard that a female preacher would be the guest speaker.

She told me later on how hard they had been praying to God for a breakthrough, for a lady pastor to come and minister the Word of God to them. (*Since women were not encouraged to preach in the district*).

The testimonies I received from them after I had left were very positive and stimulating. Pastor Andrew who invited me emailed us asking me to come back because the women needed more encouragement and the Word of God.

One incident that made me feel a bit cold was on the day I was standing on the platform and preaching. When I cast my eyes to my far left, I caught a glimpse of three male pastors chit-chatting, doing their own thing, obviously not in spirit with us. I was puzzled and disheartened, to say the least. I later discovered that they were amongst those people who begrudged having a female preacher at the meeting. And I grasped that because of them God changed the message to encourage the women to do what He Himself had called them to do. The word that came was from the book of Nehemiah. It was about when Nehemiah heard about the ruins of Jerusalem's walls, how he did what he could to help in the reconstruction process but the opposition he had to grapple with. That did not stop him; he trusted the Lord to provide and to assist him finish the wall. If God did it for Nehemiah, He did the same for me. And He will do the same for you.

In my preaching, I also spoke about the story of Ruth and Naomi. I explained how God took their hopelessness and transformed it into joy and blessings. During that service, I saw their faces lit up in faith and expectancy.

As soon as I was winding up my prayer, two gentlemen climbed up onto the podium where I was standing with a microphone. They introduced themselves as pastors from Texas, USA. Pastor Andrews had met them the day before and informed them about the forthcoming conference. So, they decided to attend the meeting, even though they missed my full preaching.

What I did not know was that God had His own idea. Those pastors were asked to come and have a word with the people. They asked us to open our Bibles to the book of Nehemiah. This got all of us rolling our eyes when he began to speak about how Nehemiah when he was faced with challenges and how God came through for him. He used almost the same words, the same tone and actions that I had used in my preaching earlier. People were screaming, shouting and thanking God. Those two pastors confirmed exactly what I had preached before.

To my surprise, those three pastors, one by one, came and asked me if I could befriend their wives and encourage them in the Lord. Our God is faithful.

On our way home I mentioned to my host pastor about what the Lord did while I was ministering; how the Lord showed me those three pastor's faces and their attitude of disunity. He then explained to me about how they despised women preachers. I was glad he did not mention that to me before I preached, because if I had heard that I am pretty sure it would have stifled my preaching and desolated me. I was glad the Lord Himself did what He did just to show people it was He who calls and decides on our destinies.

Chapter 5
THE GOMA AND UGANDA MISSION

One evening in January 2002 we were in the sitting room watching the news about Goma—how the volcano had destroyed houses, buildings and killed several people who had their houses built in its way.

All I could hear deep down my heart was a whimpering from afar: "Help! Please, help, help! I turned to my husband, who was sitting on my right, and said, "Oh, I wish we could do something to help these people." And he nodded in agreement. "We have to do something."

While we brooded on this, my phone buzzed with a call. I quickly picked it up and it was one of our pastors. In a split second, he was affirming the same words I had told my husband. By this now it had become apparent to go and assist them.

One of our mission partners had a friend who lived and had a church in Goma. According to him, they almost lost everything. I heard a voice saying "Yes, you can go and help them." Whereas we were preparing to go and donate, some organisations bigger than ours were trying to raise some big money to go and help the people of Goma. The government had given them some money to go and rescue lives.

As a small Christian charity, we decided that if God wanted us to go and help the people of Goma, we will do just that. Then suddenly, the thought kicked in: since all these big charity organisations were heading to Goma, we felt we should just donate to them as they were also going to do the same thing. However, the Lord said to me that the large organisations may have the money and the equipment, but they were not going to give the people spiritual upliftment, hence the need for us to go.

"Go and I will be your guide," The Lord said to me after a week when we began writing to some ministers to donate to assist us to make our journey to Goma. Some promised to assist but when the time came, to our astonishment, none of them sent us a penny. Those we did not contact rather blessed us with what we needed. One thing I learnt from that experience was that never put your trust in anybody just as the Bible says never trust or put your confidence in man because they will fail you.

My sisters and brothers, when God says you should do something and you find yourself in a position where there seems to be no way, know that God is in control.

Even though none of these ministers helped us on our mission trip, there was a way because Jesus had already prepared everything for us. Preaching the word to the people about the goodness of God was great. It was also great to be able to assist them in their difficult time. Whenever Jesus finishes preaching about spiritual things, He ends it with the practical. Because the practical is as significant as the theory, the prayers.

Preparation

On February 2nd we had a conference through which we were able to raise about £526. I contacted some ministers concerning our trip, which got them very excited. They said wonderful things about the trip. They asked when we were leaving, and I said in March. Some said they would see what they could do. Others made it clear that they only supported well-established, large organisations, not budding ones like ours. This was so hurting. Some also wished us the best, even though it became evident that they were not in the position to help. Some said we would hear from them, but we never heard from them.

I received a call from a man who said he wanted to know what we do, and I briefed him on what *Wood World Missions* stands for, where we have been and what we are doing. He introduced himself as a pastor from a church called Christian Family Ministries. He said he would like to support us on what we were doing because he believed that *we are doing what our Lord Jesus said we should do.* This man of God promised to donate to help our Goma trip, and he kept his promise by sending us a cheque. His name is Rev Nana Owusuh. Man of God, may the good Lord bless you.

Another sister who had been a blessing to us sent us a cheque of £100 to support the trip. The same sister brought us about 200 blankets to give to the homeless people in Goma and other parts of Africa. My dear sister, may God bless you.

We were still waiting on God for the funds He had promised us. Oasis church (Colliers Wood) also supported us with some funds to pay the shipping cost. Our Minister friends in Uganda had also arranged to rent a truck and a car to take us across from Uganda to Goma. Proverb 30:5 says "Every word of God proves true; he defends all those who came to him for protection."

I woke up to a bright and sunny day with birds chirping happily in the trees. It dawned on me that I would be flying out of the country later in the day, and so I checked my passport and other documents to be sure everything was set. I could see the sadness written all over Rev. William when he realised that it was time for me to go. He was, however, excited about my leaving to go and do God's work. We packed all bags by 4 p.m. On our way to the airport, we stopped by a supermarket to buy some spray, as it could be very hot and humid in Africa. I had already put in my luggage a range of toiletries. I was flying with a Kenya airline – flight number KQ101. After checking-in, I realised I had arrived way too early and so I waited till 7pm when boarding began. All along, my prayer was to meet a born again Christian so that we could sit together and share the gospel, and of course, meet someone I could witness to.

I said to myself, "Lord, thank you for allowing me to be a witness for you; Your word says you have given us the opportunity to be witnesses; thank you Lord for using me." Our plane was about half an hour late and while waiting, I met a lady from Uganda. It was obvious she was going on a holiday and my guess was right. She said she was a resident in London but was going home for the Easter holidays.

It was ten to eight and we were just about to take off. At that time, I had never boarded a Kenyan airline before and, my God, their service was superb. They were very affectionate and cordial. The air hostesses were efficient, and everyone had their television on the back of the seats in front of them. I said to myself "If I should visit Kenya again, I'm going to fly with their national airline."

In the plane, I sat next to a young man who was about my son's age. During our chat, I learnt his parents were Indian, a student in England who was on his way home for the Easter holidays. It was now 3am London time and almost 6am where we had reached from the small telly on the back of the seat in front of me. The journey from London to Nairobi was about eight hours, after which I would have to change flights for Uganda.

When we finally flew into Uganda, the pilot announced our landing would delay owing to air traffic and the weather condition. And so, we were going in circles for over thirty minutes. We remained in the sky for another forty minutes. And while I could not feel how windy and cold it was outside the aircraft, I cast my eyes into the clouds, adoring God's creation. Oh, it was beautiful. The mountains, the satellite view of the parks, they appeared as though I were a bird in flight.

Even though it was cloudy and windy, God calmed the winds and stopped the lightning and we landed safely in Nairobi, Kenya. This experience reminded me of Moses—he could see Canaan, but he could not get there.

Now on my way to Uganda, we waited patiently for the next plane to arrive. At the airport in Uganda, I was met by two pastors (Pastor James Mwesigwa and Pastor Charles Wilson) and one of the elders of the church. I was asked to preach at their church an hour after I had landed. The church was thronged with people—a vibrant and lively church. As usual, I could not hide my ecstasy, I burst into dancing. God gave me a special anointing to preach even though I was jet-lagged—having flown for thirteen hours—from London to Kenya and then to Uganda.

After the service, we were invited to the pastor's house for a meal. We ate Matooke, a delicious local dish with stew, rice, boiled ripe plantain. We chatted for about three hours before going home. After twenty-three hours since I left London, I had finally had an hour rest before the next meeting with another pastor on how we could transport the goods to Goma from the airport. I was told it will cost £25 or more a day until the truck reached Goma, a journey of two to three days.

Then the day arrived, and we were on our way to the airport to clear the goods. Before we could pay for the goods, we needed to change some money. At the airport, we were told that we could not take the goods because the truck owner was unavailable. I was beginning to understand the principles of monopoly. No other truck goes to the place where we were supposed to transfer the goods to. We had to wait another day or pay an extra 300 Ugandan money for the service.

We left the airport gorgeously disappointed and displeased yet convinced in our hearts that God was in control. Rev. William called to assure me that everything would be okay. His calls always come at the right time, which always tell me that I married a man after God's own heart—a man so in love with God.

We waited patiently for a call from the airport to let us know when we could collect our goods, but we did not receive the call. What is going on? I thought.

Our God is good, I assured myself, He will come through for us. There must be a reason for this delay. Pastor Charles called while I was praying, he was trying to get a reasonable price for the truck to Goma.

At about 5:30 p.m. I was preaching at the Faith Arena. I had prepared a sermon, but the Holy Spirit gave me a *Word* for the season and directed me to the book of Mark 5:1-43. While preaching, I called for those with alcoholic problems and many of them were delivered. The spirit led me to prophesy to some other people who were present at the meeting.

After the message, there were many testimonies and people were saved from all kinds of addictions. Praise be to God. There was one particular man, a pastor, who confessed that he was possessed by demons. He stopped preaching and started drinking heavily, and womanising. He had not been to church for two years, but he somehow turned up to church on that day — praise God. You can imagine how his mum felt—she was overjoyed to see his prodigal son come home, healed.

Another testimony was about a man who came to the service wallowing in frustration, so he wanted to excuse himself outside, as he felt he did not belong there.

On his way out, I called him back. During the service, I asked him to come in front and introduce himself. He said his name was Daniel. I immediately sensed in the spirit that he was a man of God and a prophet. The word came to me that God was going to use him mightily. I also saw in the spirit realm many problems he was facing in his life and when I relayed the message to him, he nodded in agreement, pleading with me to pray for him.

Daniel was shocked and everyone was clapping and cheering for his deliverance – this man of God had churches with faithful members. You could just imagine that the pastor was pleased to know that God had sent a servant from London to deliver him. God works in mysterious ways.

We prayed for Pastor Daniel and he went home with his shoulders held high and his faith whole. It became clear to me why we had the delay – God wanted to rescue and deliver his people. We serve an awesome God; He is the living God. Thank you, Father, for making a way and blessing your people in Goma.

At about 10pm Rev. William called me; we chatted for about 30 minutes before I went to bed. He told me everyone was praying for me. God is indeed good – no fears; He will answer our prayers. Pastor Charles called and promised to meet us the following morning.

God is in control

The following day, my prayer was: "Good morning God, I know that you are always in control. We will be going to the airport this morning to see the commissioner about how we can get the goods out today, I know *You are in Control.*"

At 9 am, I had just finished worshipping and praising God. We waited for the rest of the team to arrive home before leaving for the airport. We met William the clearing agent. He and brother Tom, another agent, bargained as much as they could for us to get a reasonable fare to Goma.

It was now about 4:30 pm. "Lord, let Your will be done" was my prayer. Just as we thought all hope was gone, we were approached by another person waiting to send his pharmaceutical drugs to Goma.

Yes, God was opening the doors for us. Instead of one person to share with, we now had an additional three Christian brothers and sisters to travel with because the road was dangerous for one driver. We paid the special fare for protection. "Lord, thank you," we said, "Indeed, you are a good God; where there is no way, you always make a way."

Sometimes it looks like the way is completely blocked, but then he who has begun a good work in us will always complete it. God works in a way we cannot imagine or understand. He always prepares a way for his children. We met some people at the airport while discussing what to do next.

It happened that all those people the Lord brought our way were Christians. Pastor Richard from Victory Ministries Kampala assisted in handling our goods and showing us around. Another brother also helped us to find a truck that goes to the border of Zaire.

We were greatly assisted by other brethren and we are grateful to them for their help and assistance. Our God was in control. He brought Christian brethren to help us. All I could say was, "Oh God, you are good." God directed our affairs because we did commit everything to Him. Sister Margaret is a church member of Faith Arena, who became my assistant, helping me, cooking and taking care of the household chores in Kampala. The waiting game was taking its toll on us, but we were still smiling. "How are you doing?" asked Brother Willie the driver. "Well, I am okay," I replied.

"You seem so joyful despite the delays." He said.

"Yes, because God is watching over the situation so I do not need to worry myself; my God has already promised that everything will be alright. However, thank you for asking." I replied.

The day was almost over, but we were not getting anywhere with the paperwork. It was nearly 5pm, around the same time the offices closed. "Lord, I need you at this moment to make a way," I whispered prayerfully to myself. Your actions in times of trouble always show who you are in Christ.

I have been preaching and encouraging people on how to stand and trust God and that He will answer them when they call. This was my turn to do the same thing and I knew that I had to trust God even when it seemed too lonely. I prayed and suddenly I was calm and elated. I said, "Hey guys, let's stand still and see the salvation of our God."

At that very moment Pastor Charles gave me a big smile and said, "Rev. Mercy, everything is okay now. We have to go to Nakawa in the morning to clear the papers with the Customs officers before we can take the goods."

Day 6

God is good. The sixth day was wonderful. The rains had stopped, and the floodwaters had receded. We were about to set off to *Nakawa depot* for all the goods. It was now 10am and we were in the town centre. I went and emailed my husband to inform him where we were and the outcome of the previous day. I know they were praying for me at church back in London. I knew individuals were also praying for me from across the globe. At about 12pm we arrived at Nakawa to finalise the paperwork. By 4pm we had received all the documents and, hey, we were on our way to Goma. Hurray!!

Jesus & Me on the Road to Goma

We came back to Kampala to book our transport. We would be leaving Kampala at 4am and we needed to be at the station before 4am otherwise we would miss the bus. At 3am I was awake, I could not sleep. I had been told that I needed to have a good bath because it would take 2 solid days to reach our destination.

We arrived at the bus stop. The bus was so crammed. How am I going to stretch my legs? I said. I had no choice. There was no other way to get to Goma unless I was prepared to foot another hundred pounds just for my convenience. If I had decided to carry my cross and follow Jesus, I must as well keep silent in my uncomfortable situation. I focused on what Jesus endured for my sake and endured my inconvenience. The driver was driving at a fast speed despite the bad and rough road. We stopped at a small village because these buses only pass these villages just once in a day, so if you missed it you would have to wait for another day.

What an inconvenience! They also charged exorbitant fares. *Take it or live it* was their motto. Not all of us could fit into the truck, so Pastor Charles went along with the other convoy.

We were now halfway to the border between Uganda & Zaire. It was getting dark and we needed to get to the border and report before 6pm; we were nowhere near the border. Luckily, we had already paid two police escorts to accompany us so that we do not get any surprise attacks! "Lord, we have gone so far, no turning back. We will get there because you are with us," I continued to pray.

Some parts of the road were rugged and scary – valleys, mountains, animals crossing, humans crossing – a multitude of things happening all at the same time. Amidst the chaos, I noticed a beautiful deep valley that reminded me of the songs that we sometimes sing at church.

> *"On the mountains, in the valley,*
>
> *on the land and in the sea.*
>
> *The Lord is my portion*
>
> *in the land of the living*
>
> *my God is good forevermore."*

This was an experience. The mountain was so high and the valley so deep. It was so scary and on top of that, we passed through a small old bridge that looked like it was going to break at any time. Some parts were coiled and narrow. "What an adventure," I said to Pastor James Mwesigwa.

Here comes the interesting part. After many hours travelling on the road, we reached a village called Hikiki and the bus stopped. But we remained on the vehicle, yearning to bring the long journey to an end. We waited for about ten minutes when someone asked us why we were still on the bus. I said that we are waiting for the driver to take us to the border between Uganda & Zaire. The man said "No, no lady! This is where we stop. You all have to get off."

"How are we going to get to the border?" I asked.

"That's not my problem, lady," he said.

"What can we do, we cannot walk from here. On top of that, it is about 5:30pm and we only have 30 minutes to get to the border before it closes." I said.

"Well, the only way you can get there is to take a motorcycle called 'border- border'." He said.

We could not have walked either because from Hikiki to the border was about 8 to 10 Kilometres. "Motorbike!" I screamed, "The last time I sat on a motorbike was in 1978."

"Well sister, you have no choice, motorbike or walk because you have no choice." The man continued. Oh my God, I whispered. Lord help us, Apostles mumbled.

"Okay," I said, looking at Pastor James in awe. He was comfortable in using motorbikes (Border-Border) because it made life easier for them to visit the villages not roadworthy.

Did I have a choice? Border-Border or I walk. In desperation, I sat on the back of this little motorbike driven by a young man of about 20 years old. The journey took us between 30 to 40 minutes. We arrived only to find out we could not cross the border until the next day. Oh, what an adventure! Everything that could go wrong had gone wrong, but my God was still in control. We shall cross the line.

We arrived at the national Game Park with the entire animal kingdom around us. We booked to stay in one of the hotels. I had a tiny room with a mosquito net to stop them feasting on me. After checking in, we went out for a walk – we needed some exercise after the long journey. We were told to be careful as there were lions and other dangerous animals about. Yes indeed, we saw different species of monkeys. We later found something to eat, had a bath then went to bed. My Lord, I know you are with me on this journey, I sighed.

Saturday 23rd March 2002

Today was a week since I left my family, friends and others to go on this missionary trip. We faced many hurdles and the vicissitudes of life, but we overcame all obstacles by the grace of the Lord. We woke up the following morning with a hullabaloo, it was a chimpanzee flexing his muscles and demanding bananas. It dawned on us that we are staying in a park full of animals, all types and sizes. You cannot go out during the dark otherwise you may come face-to-face with wild animals.

There were big and small monkeys at the back of the house. I was told they would approach me if I was wearing a straight dress. They would avoid me if I wore trousers because they do not like men, they believe that men would snatch their babies. Those who came were female chimps and monkeys.

It was now almost 9am and I was getting ready to go to the border to get an update. God will make way for us. Our truck driver was very funny; he told many jokes and lifted our spirits. He was an experienced driver doing at least 3 trips a week from Congo to Uganda, Kenya, Tanzania. He told us that because of poverty some of the guards would deliberately obstruct and delay their trips. The way around this problem was to offer them inducements. This is what he said, "My sister, this place is so dry, so is their pocket." When they see a foreigner, it makes their day. There was no light, telephone, or television. We were in the middle of a forest, a national park. Oh, what an adventure it was.

Press On

It was now 11am. "We were still waiting for our documents to come from another town," said the customs officer. Our other problem was just solved. One of our team members left his passport at home so at the border he had to complete a temporary passport and put his photograph on it to enable him to enter the Congo. Luckily, he had a picture and the immigration officer, too, was kind and caring, so he allowed him to cross the border. As we were waiting, at around noon, we were informed that the documents would arrive by 3pm. By the grace of the Lord, we would leave the border before 6pm otherwise we couldn't cross to the other side.

This reminded me of Paul's journey when he encountered many problems on his journeys, but in all his difficulties God was with him. We pressed on with faith.

Now the same God was still with us. I learnt to eat food I never thought I could eat. I learnt to sleep in a small room with just a bed, a room with mosquito blood smeared on the walls and cobwebs in the ceiling. Our bathroom was shared with other people at the same time. The toilet was outside. You can imagine what happened at night when one wanted to visit the toilet. This is what mission work is all about. The day before, we only had bread and water all day till 8pm; we had some soup called 'stew'. Had I got a choice? Certainly not. I ate it because I was hungry and besides there was nowhere to buy anything in the jungle. Jesus said, "Go ye therefore," so I go wherever he sends me. The army officers were nice and sympathetic towards us. One of them said I should eat everything I could eat since we had 120km to go after we had checked out at Isha-sha.

"My Lord will make a way," I said to myself. Now the day was almost over; we had just finished at the border, but it was too late to travel that night even though it was about 5pm. They had informed us nobody could travel on such a road in the night. Unfortunately, we had to stay in the jungle again. We could hear the soothing orchestra of animals. Using that as a caution, one of the guards told us not to go out after 6.30 pm. This was because the lions and the tigers would come out at night. There were many deer and monkeys around the village. I want to tell you something interesting and funny that happened to me that night.

Around 3am I needed to use the toilet. I was desperate. The whole place was quiet, and everyone was in their rooms. The toilet was outside the compound. I had to spend this penny now! I desperately needed to spend a penny, but I was scared because those wild animals were still around as it was dark. Oh boy, what should I do? Lord, please help me out! I stood outside my door hoping someone would come out at the same time so that we could go together, but no one came. I crept back to bed. I could not even sleep. I began to pray. As I was praying, I fell into a deep sleep. I woke up at about 5am and no one was out yet. So, I said, "Lord come with me, I need to go, otherwise, I will wet myself in bed or hurt my kidney if I hold it too long." I took my small torchlight, opened the gate to the bush and quickly relieved myself. It was only when I was coming out that I saw another person. I bet we were in the same boat. He was waiting for someone to come out, too. Strangely, it was a man.

The people there never get up until 7am. I mean the whole village at least till 6:30am. What an amazing adventure that was. I was looking forward to hopefully going through the border to a small village in Zaire, which is called *No Man's Land*, and through the national park. I was looking forward to us continuing our journey.

Sunday 24th March 2002

Day 9

It had now been three days since we left Kampala. We needed to go through part of Rwanda and then to Goma. We had now finished with the customs offices in Ishasha, Uganda border. We were now entering the Congo border. This was another hurdle to endure.

We were told I had to pay $60 for my visa and the two Pastors had to pay $30 each. They had no money. It was all down to me to pay for it. I haggled with them because I couldn't understand why I should pay that amount for visas. I thought you only paid for just once which I had done already. They later agreed and I paid total of $30.

My other problem now was how to transport the goods to Goma because the other lorry was not allowed to cross the border. While waiting, we decided to find a church to go to. The church was called 'Community Baptist Church', which was really nice because I was not expecting to see a church in that small village. We took a picture with the Pastor.

We, in fact, were the first foreigners to visit that church, as I was told. You can imagine the joy we brought to the church. By the way, we were still waiting, this time waiting at the Congo side of the border.

The message for the day at the church was quoted from Mathew and Hebrews:

Matthew 28: 18-20: *"All power given unto me in heaven and into the earth, go ye therefore and teach all nations, baptizing them, in the name of the father, the son and of the Holy Ghost. Teaching them to observe all things whatsoever I have commanded you and low, I am with you always even unto the end of the world."*

Hebrews 13: 1 *"Let brotherly love continue"*.

These two verses inspired me so much. It felt like "God, we are doing the work you said we should do, but here we are on a mission trip in the jungle with different cultures and people who can't speak English." There was a communication barrier. I thank God I persevered because He is my guardian. I may be powerless to do whatsoever, but I know God is with me.

We shall go to Goma no matter what. For the last 4 days, we had not eaten a proper meal. We had been living on bread, water and peanuts. "Lord, please move once again so that we can have a proper meal." Our last four slices of bread were stolen by baboons (monkeys) at the border while we were discussing what to do next. Very funny, isn't it?

I really wondered how the Apostles coped when they were going to places to preach the gospel. The walking, the blockages, the uncertainties, you name it. If we didn't get any bus today before 4pm it meant we had to sleep again in Isha-shah. Well, maybe God has some work for us to do here, who knows. All I kept hearing from people was, "why don't you give up and go back to where you came from! It's not easy to get to Goma, there are many obstacles on your way. Just give the donations and items to us here and go back home; tell everybody you have been to Goma."

Can you imagine the temptation? It seemed easy to give up and turn back without accomplishing the task. My reply to them was "God will make a way. I did not come this far to give up, that is not my style, no matter what."

We had to go through ten or so smaller villages before we got to Goma. According to the map I saw, Lava had wiped most of the city. I was told that most of the people and many things got buried. It was now 2pm according to Congo time. We needed God to move his hands on us before 4pm because we did not want to sleep in that village one more night.

Shortly after that, I saw the bus coming. "Hurry, our bus has come," I told my team. Meanwhile, here was one of the officers asking me to pay $120 before taking the goods to Goma. "What! What for? And why did I ask? Because I had already paid for the declarations at the airport before coming.

"You need to pay for customs checks. This is Congo," he said, "as a visitor, you have to comply with the rules and regulations."

I insisted I had no money on me, that I was broke. I told him, "I haven't eaten for days and you are asking me to pay more money. These goods are for charity; free items for distribution in Goma. I am not going to sell and get profit out of it. This is to help the needy that are suffering. And you are making my life more miserable, adding to my discomfort."

After pleading with them for several hours, they agreed that I should go with one police escort and customs officer. The agreement was that I had to pay for their upkeep until we reached Goma.

To my surprise, the police and the customs officer were of no help at all. They were an inconvenience to us. We were clamped in the van and on top of that the policeman was smoking like a chimney.

Despite the presence of the police and the customs officer, I was compelled to go through another customs check and pay another fee, we had to use the very last penny on us. Once that was done, we drove off.

"Oh, thank God, we are on our way now," I said. The road was bad and very undulating. "How long will it take before we arrive?" I asked. The driver said we had to stop and park and sleep. I asked why. The driver said there was a roadblock and we could not continue. And so here we were in the jungle. With no more money left on us because we had spent it all on transportation and unnecessary taxations.

We spent 3 days at the border. There were so many borders. I had never gone through so many borders in my life. At each border, we had to pay the officers as they whined about not having any fixed income. For this, they perceived us as preys, and it did not matter to them whether we had money or not. To their mind, my being a foreigner meant I needed to have money. And when I pondered this, it broke my heart. I could imagine how devastating and stringent it was for our brethren who first took the gospel to these remote places. I was experiencing the same situation in Congo. Everything was about money. If you did not have money, you could not do anything.

We eventually found somewhere safe to park for the night. We slept in the van with our goods, without food, thankfully we had water. We prayed over the bottles of water before gulping it. Near the car was a lady cooking. We could smell the aroma, but we could not buy any. I was seated in the front seat with Pastor James inhaling the aroma and praying God would use it to satisfy me. Pastor Charles had sandwiched himself in the back with the rest with his nose poked in the air probably imitating me. I smiled and said it is well. He smiled back and said amen. God will feed us. I sat and slept at the same spot. It was hard to turn myself around to relax.

At around 2am, I needed to use the toilet. Outside was very cold and scary, especially when you turned your mind to the roaring, howling, mooing emanating from the nearby forest. But I needed to pee, so I held the front door open and stepped out into the pitch darkness. No one was awake, I did not want to bother them. I wanted them to have some rest so they could have the strength to continue the journey early morning. I sauntered to the house where the woman was cooking last night. I was told that place was supposed to be a hotel. I was startled to find the toilet seat right next to the bucket of water they were using to cook the food. I mumbled to myself, how awful, how disgusting. I thanked God we were broke; otherwise, we would have bought the food, considering the rumblings in our stomachs. The bathroom and the toilet were in the same place where they fetched their drinking and cooking water. My stomach started to churn as I continued to look around. Thank God we survived that awful night. We began praying to the Lord with songs of praises and worship in the morning. Oh, it was wonderful!

The Situation in Goma and the Blessed Blankets

Monday, 25th March 2002

Day 10

"Good morning, hey! We are alive, and our goods are also here. Thank God for protecting us," I said to them. The time was 6am and we had to set off.

On our way, we were stopped several times by the police. The first incident was the police finding out that the driver did not have insurance and the van had not been insured to travel for a long journey. They insisted that we get one before proceeding with the journey. They showed us where to secure it, we went to get one really quick and continued the journey. We hardly travelled 2km when other police officers stopped us. This time they were asking for money since we had provided all the right travel documents. With God's grace and love, we arrived safely in Goma. Praise God.

The Situation in Goma

The volcano had caused a lot of damage in Goma. Almost the whole airport was obliterated. Some repairs and renovations were being done. Half of the city was now in ruins. The refugees lived in very tiny grass houses with their families. Standing by the volcano remains, it was like watching a film made in Hollywood, but this was for real this time. Smoke was still coming through the Lava, I touched it and it was still hot.

This was an adventure and also a testimony for me, God always works in mysterious ways. All the problems we faced on our way to Goma, the difficulties, the delays were worth the journey. This mission trip has taught me a lot of lessons about the real Christian commission.

Staying in a comfortable church or preaching in cities and towns with all the trimmings does not really show the real nature of what the Lord said we should do. The real message or job is to go to places such as Goma or such villages preaching as well as city missions. For two days we had not eaten any proper meal except water. We had no money left but miraculously we found 1000 Rwanda shilling (10 pence), which we used to buy sugarcane, which became a lifesaver since we lost our only bread to the monkeys. It was rather funny the way the monkeys snatched the bread from my hands. It was a Sunday morning at a place called isha-sha. Hopefully tonight we shall have real solid food, I said.

Journey through Rwanda

Passing through Rwanda was rather very scary because we could see the military gorillas with their guns everywhere; from Isha-sha right through to Goma. I am talking about 120km drive or more on rough and dangerous roads. Just about 2km from a village (refugee camp), we could see the havoc caused by the volcano. Looking at the ruins, you could actually see how the lava had spread like a carpet or like a tractor had cleared the whole village. It was unbelievable! We saw a big Catholic Church that had sunk and was burnt. One of the eyewitnesses narrated the story to us saying: "The lava first burst out of the small mountain and then disappeared not knowing that it had gone underground." Shortly after, they saw a sudden eruption near a small-town centre taking everything, buildings, cars, animals, vegetation, everything on its path. "We witnessed the damage caused by the volcano; it took the whole village in a storm, killing about 120 people at once. The lava sneaked into people's houses, killing them; there was no time for them to park their bags or save their lives."

This example shows how the devil sneaks into people's lives and before they can realise he has already done the damage in their lives, just like what Jesus said in John 10:10: The thief (devil) purpose is to steal, to kill and to destroy; Jesus' purpose is to give life in its fullness." (NIV).

Even though our trip was very tiring and very frustrating, the Lord allowed us to share the gospel. People were asking me how I managed to cope with the situation. I told them that because of God, I overcame it. There is no victory without a battle. Imagine travelling for days without food, but still smiling and looking good and fresh. I can tell you God is good. The gospel of our Lord Jesus Christ will be preached everywhere. The Lord has ordained it to be preached. It is not going to be easy but with Him on our side, we can do all things.

This mission trip allowed me to meet people from different cultures and professional backgrounds. I met ministers of God, ministers of the government, immigration and customs officers, you name them.

Pastor Lukoo, who happened to be my host organised a meal for my team and I. He took us to some spots where the volcano had started. According to Pastor Lukoo, some of the members who were working in the centre, teaching in a school and such places had lost so many things. You can imagine the agony and the frustration they were contending with.

The night before we reached our destination, it reminded me of Peter sleeping in a dirty uncomfortable prison and the Lord sending angels to set him free. I had a dream that a man came asking for more money from us. I said to him I did not have any money to give him. I woke up thinking hunger might have incited the dream but surprisingly it was a real dream. Because as soon as I thought everything was over, I was told somebody wanted to see me.

Strangely enough, he happened to be the man I saw in the dream. It was the police escort who came in the van with us. I could not believe my ears and eyes after all that I went through. He had the nerve to ask for more money. In the end, he decided he wanted a blanket for his family. In my generosity, I gave him two blankets.

I could not imagine this man pursuing us because of blankets. These blankets, which were originally called the unwanted waste of space blankets, now had become so needful, a celebrity.

That said, let me give you the pleasure of reading what a friend & a partner of WWM, who donated these blankets, had to say. I believe it would encourage you, just in case you have been told you are useless or a waste of space.

"Blessed Blankets"

by Dorothy Cromwell

This is the story of the blessed blankets

"I heard about Wood World Missions when I came to Oasis Church in 2001. I wanted to support it because it is a small mission going where the larger organisations cannot always reach. It also ministers to the whole person giving aid and the gospel.

I work in a large Nursing Home and sometimes clothes are donated to the Home, but sometimes there are too many for them to use. Just before Christmas, I was told to get rid of some unwanted clothes. "Just throw them away," someone had suggested. As there were a lot of coats and warm clothing, I gave them to a friend who was going to Poland because they needed it over there. In the New Year, I asked someone if there were any more clothes available that I could have for *Wood World Missions*. For some weeks I heard nothing so I decided I would ask the manager. She said to me "Oh, you've come about the blankets." I said, "What blankets?" She took me to the laundry room and showed me 84 blankets. All of them were in good condition and some were brand new. Apparently, they had desperately tried to give them away to charities in October, but nobody had wanted them. Mercy had told me that she was going to Goma soon and the people there had lost everything. Even a few blankets would be a blessing. When I went to the laundry room to collect the blankets, I discovered that there were many cupboards full of blankets. In my diary that day I wrote *'there may be as many as 200'*.

In fact, the total number of blankets was almost 300. God had truly multiplied them. He is a God of abundance. He never does things "by half" although he does want us to give our little to him so that He can multiply it. He wants us to be involved in what he is doing.

When we went to the WWM meeting, we were blessed and touched to see the video of the Goma trip. We saw blankets being given out in that little church halfway across the world. These blankets had cluttered our living room and had been dumped in and out of our car. Yes! It was an amazing moment. Praise God! I also want to give thanks to the Nursing Home staff for their help and support. The Home is a registered charity themselves, so we were happy to help.

I would like to share something with you. I had to make several trips to collect all the blankets. On one of my trips to the laundry room, I noticed one of the staff had written a label on the cupboards: "blinking blankets". What he meant was these blankets were a nuisance and a waste of space. I said no, these were blessed blankets. I put my hands on them and prayed over them. Then the Lord spoke clearly to me. He said we could be like those blankets. We can feel that we are washed, packed and ready to go to do great things for God.

Then we can feel as if we are shoved in a cupboard. We may be insignificant to some people because they cannot see our particular God-given gifts, nor would they recognise our potential of what we can achieve. Maybe people have said to you in the past you are a waste of space. So, we can feel we are in a dark cupboard just taking up space. Our Heavenly Father wants us to know, first we are chosen by Him, and secondly to be a blessing to Him. Also, God is saying the reason you may have had to wait is that the plan God has for your life is bigger than you first thought. Like the blankets, God wants to send us to the nations. Those blankets were handpicked by God and destined to be a blessing for the people of Goma. You are handpicked by God and destined to be a blessing. He also said do not forget the nations are here in London, too. You may feel forgotten or not appreciated but be at peace, you are in God's perfect timing. This is your time. His plan is perfect; it is to bless you and to make you a blessing.

Ephesians 1 says *"It is in Christ that we find out who we are and what we are living for. Long before we first heard of Christ and got our hopes up, he had his eye on us, had designs on us for glorious living, part of the overall purpose*

He is working out in everything and everyone". (The Message Translation).

Hebrews 10 verse 35 and 36 and Hebrews 11 verse 1 says *"So do not throw away your confidence; it will be richly rewarded. You need to persevere so that when you have done the will of God you will receive what he has promised. Now faith is being sure of what we hope for and certain of what we do not see".* (N.I.V.)

Thank you, Minister Dorothy Cromwell, for sharing this incredible story of "The Blessed Blankets". Thank God for His Mercies. What nobody wants, God can use for His glory. I can tell you these blankets have done wonders. Some went to Ghana, Ethiopia, Malawi as well as Congo.

26th March 2002

Day 11

On the second day of the lava inspection, there was still smoke all over the places. You could literally see holes as deep as 50 metres down; we saw the catastrophe of the whole place where the lava entered the lake, what it took with it was so amazing to watch. We were walking on top of the houses, tower buildings that had sunk down into the earth with the lava. Thereafter, we were taken to the

Pastor's house to have something to eat and later on we went to church. His house was just near the church.

The Pastors' house was really in a sorry state. You would cry if you saw the Pastors' dwelling place. It was made of wood and was covered with plastic and nylon carpet on the walls. It had so many holes and I wondered how he coped with the situation especially when it heavily rained with his family in there.

The pastor was very humble and was very much respected by everyone. Oh, I wish I had money to help him put up a proper house. The people also had a feeling that I was an answer to their prayers. It was Easter time, but the parents could not afford to buy anything for the children and themselves. So, my coming with clothes, blankets, shoes, toys etcetera was like manna from heaven to them. They believed God had heard their cry and had answered them.

While at the church, there were no instruments except hand-made drums and "Conga", no microphone and all of that, yet the praise and worship were very good and joyful. The church was packed full of people, some standing outside because there were no chairs left. It was a blessed day indeed.

Soon after the praise and worship, I was called to preach. God moved mightily; many people gave their lives to the Lord. Most of the children were touched by the messages so much that they came forward to give their lives to Christ. Somehow, the leaders wanted to stop them. But I explained to them that these are our future generation and they needed to stay with the Lord at that age so that they would not depart from him - Joshua 1:8.

The messages I preached, unfortunately, were not recorded on tape or video. It would have been nice to hear some of the testimonies because of the messages I preached to them. I recall one woman testified that before she came to the meeting, her head was spinning with a headache. While I was preaching and binding any sicknesses, she said she felt relieved and the pain disappeared from her. All Praise be to God. Another said that she was feeling uncomfortable with stomach pain, which disappeared when I prayed for her, Praise the Lord.

Miraculously, I felt a sharp pain on my right hip side, so I asked if anyone felt the same. More than 20 people came forward for prayers. After the prayers, some testified that the pain had gone, and they felt better. Praise God.

The pastors were so glad because they said the message I brought them was what they really needed, especially after what they had gone through. My message was taken from Act 3 and Act 4 about the prison experience.

After the service, we went home but still, people followed us to the house. I tell you these people could pray.

From my observation, I wished those of us in the west could dedicate as much time for praying as the Christians in Africa. People told us their testimonies during the volcano experience. One of them had this to say:

"I was in my room when I heard something like a bomb blast, heard people shouting, so we came out and saw fire on the mountain. We went back to the house and only to be told the volcano had erupted. Where should we go, God! But on the radio, they were told not to go anywhere. But people were running toward the border of Rwanda and everywhere just to save their lives. We found nowhere safe to go. In desperation, we returned to Goma town only to find out that everything was gone. All the big shops, schools, banks had disappeared. Where could we go then, we asked ourselves! Some of our people received help from other organisations but not everybody got some of the things they came to donate.

We helped and encouraged each other to pray to God to send anybody to help. And that is why you are here. God is good! God is good!"

There were other testimonies similar to what this lady has just shared.

While the volcanic eruption was going on, they did not know where to run to; in front of them was a hot boiling lake, and behind them was the lava flowing towards them. Some decided to stay put, holding each other's hand and praying, trusting God to save them. They felt like the days of Moses and the Israelites trapped between the red sea and the Egyptians who were chasing them. If we go the lake would swallow us and if we don't go the lava would burn us alive. What should we do? They decided to trust God and see the salvation of the Lord. And yes, indeed He did it. God can do anything at any time.

The woman said that due to the destruction, there was no food in the house. They could not even buy because the market was gone. But just in front of them, the lake brought a lot of cooked dirty fish, and they were told not to touch it because they were poisonous, but because they had no choice, they prayed, sanctified it and ate it but by the grace of God nothing happened to them just as the Bible promised in Luke 10:19.

Goma is a town with mountains and many valleys. Valleys have turned into mountains and even the lake has become big now. These people were hungry for the Word of the Lord. Thank God for making it possible for me to go to Goma to bless them both spiritually and materially. Obeying God's words to undertake mission work could take you to many places.

The Donation to the Church

Wednesday, 27th March 2002

Day 12

I had a very interesting experience that night. I could not close my eyes and sleep. Because in the house where I was lodging, there was a one-year-old baby who kept us awake with his incessant crying. I was sharing a bed with her mum and her daughter. Brothers and sisters, if you are thinking of doing missionary work, please be prepared for any surprises and be prepared to give up your comfort zone. The baby cried half of the night until 6 a.m. What a night!

This house has only two bedrooms with seven children including their mother, and father, myself, pastor Charles and Pastor James. They, too, shared one small room - 12 of us were sleeping under one roof. They really tried their best to look after us, despite our uncomfortable sleepless nights.

Day 13

Looking at my watch, it said 4am. I shut my eyes again. I had to wake up between 5am and 6am. When I woke up, I said my prayers, went straight to the bathroom. I could feel the dizziness in my eyes, but I could not sleep. We were travelling back to Kampala and we needed to catch a bus to a certain town called Gunaguma near Rwanda – between Zaire and Uganda border. We boarded another bus to a town called Kisoro where we slept for the night.

At about 2am when we were having a deep and satisfying slumber, they shouted at us to wake up and get ready. *Oh no, 2am - we only went to bed at 12am*, I sighed. We had gone to bed late because we were praying and sharing the word.

There was no time for a shower, so I got up, washed my face and put on spray and deodorant. I was informed we needed to board the bus by 3am because it would leave at 4am. If we missed the bus, that meant we would have to wait for another day and if it was fully booked then we were in trouble. I really did miss my family but could not do anything about it due to lack of network and money. I had not spoken to them for a whole week.

The Lord said if you have to take up your cross and follow Him according to Mark 8:34, it would cost you your comfort, your time, your pleasures and your money. It costs to follow Christ but there is peace and joy when we faithfully do his work.

Missionary duty was and still is a wonderful thing to do if you have been called to do so. Travelling to unknown countries, eating unknown food, crossing borders, meeting with strange people, some horrible, some kind, some who want to dupe you - you have to cope with these challenges. I thank God for all those who did pray for me. Sometimes the challenges were overwhelming, but we focused our eyes on the Lord and He saw us through. There were times when it seemed all hope had gone but then God steps in and directs our affairs.

For instance, Thursday the 23rd March 2002 was a typical example. we ran out of money, yet we had 480km to get back to Kampala. God provided for us to pay for our trip. Pastor Charles said before we left Uganda that he felt he needed to take his mobile phone with him but didn't tell us why. Not knowing God had a plan for that phone at a crucial time when we would need it. He sacrificed his precious possession and he sold it in Goma to a wealthy man so that we could go back to Kampala. He only told us what he did after he had sold it. God is our provider; He shall never leave us nor forsake us.

Coming back from Goma was a little bit better compared to the Isha-sha route where we had many things to carry. We passed through another easy route, which was dangerous but a bit better than the other side because the immigration officers were nicer and friendly. The Lodge where we stayed was not bad though we had to use bathroom facilities outside the room. It was communal use – both bathroom and toilet. The unpleasant odour was terrible. I do not have to give you all the details; I leave the rest to your imagination.

The only thing I missed out on was the monkeys who were ravaging the house and compound looking for food. Thank God they did not harm anyone. I was also told that if you attack any one of them, the whole family of monkeys would descend upon you and try to seek revenge for attacking a member of their family. The same is true of our Heavenly Father, anyone who attacks His children would be punished.

I am so glad that the Lord has given me the opportunity to share the gospel. I am not ashamed to share the gospel of Christ which is our salvation.

Like Apostle Paul said in 1 Corinthians 9:16 *"I am compelled to preach. Woe to me if I do not preach the gospel."* And in verses 17 he continued *"If I were volunteering the services at my own free will, then the Lord would give me a special reward; but that is not the situation, for God has picked me out and given me this sacred trust, and I have no choice."* NIV.

As followers of Christ, we need to give up some of our possessions, our time and other comforts so that we can fulfil the great commission that Jesus entrusted into our hands. Pastor Charles and Pastor James, from Uganda, gave up their lives, time and comfort, to travel with me. Pastor Charles sold his precious possession (a mobile phone which somebody donated to him from abroad) to enable us to get back from Kampala to Zaire.

To me, this was a sacrifice, because for someone to sell his mobile phone in Africa to assist the work of God is not a mere task. Mobile phones are special commodities to have, especially in Africa, where not as many people can afford them. That did not stop him from parting with it for us. Besides, something happened at Kisoro according to Pastor Charles, during the night as they departed from my room after prayer; he heard the knock on the door and asked who it was. 'It's the Police!" replied the voice.

He demanded to know what we were doing in that village and where we came from. He explained that we were missionaries eager to spread the gospel of Christ. There was a heavy presence of the police and soldiers in the rural areas to prevent fighting against warring factions. Strangers were usually questioned to ascertain their motives.

Seven days in the jungles and wilderness had really opened my spiritual mind about the work of God. I was so glad that the Lord brought us out of dangerous situations and guided us through the journey. I believe that the prayers and intercessions of our friends and partners greatly assisted us in our travels.

I will continue to obey God and preach the Gospel of our Lord Jesus Christ until He calls me home. For me doing God's will and work is the most important thing in my life. God did not spare His own Son but gave Him up for us. He did not hold anything back from us. He gave us His most precious gift (Jesus Christ) and including the spiritual gifts He has given us all. Since God had held nothing back from us, He expects that we will hold nothing back from Him.

He has given us something precious and great, we too must give ourselves to Him by doing His will. Jesus said we should go into the world, preach the Gospel, and help the needy. In doing so, He will be with us no matter what we may face. He would be with us even to the end.

I remember laying down on my bed at the village lodge which they called the hotel and I felt the Lord saying to me: "Mercy, I am with you through this missionary journey, though the jungles, volcanoes, mountains and treacherous places; I will protect you from any harm because you have laid down your comfort zone to help those destitute people who were are in need and also preach my word."

At that moment, the thought that came to my mind was the story of Paul facing so many challenges but, in my case, there were no beatings on my back. However, my journey felt like Paul's shipwreck experience. Mountains and Valleys.

Friday 29th March

Day 14

Thank you, Lord, for taking me out of my comfort zone and using me to be a blessing to people around the world.

Our bus was speeding so fast on the bad roads by the mountains and very deep valleys. The place was full of fog; you could hardly see but the driver seemed to know what he was doing. We almost had a serious crash between the mountain and the valley because a passing lorry came around the bent very fast and almost hit our vehicle, but God was in control.

As we drove about 4 kilometres, we witnessed an accident. A petrol tanker went into the ditch, another bus full of people had a crush and, unfortunately, many people died.

Our bus arrived in Kampala a bit earlier than I imagined. Everybody was waiting for us; they had been praying; they hadn't heard from us for a long time and they had become concerned. Within three hours after I had arrived, I was preaching at an all-night prayer meeting until 5.30am. My message for the night was: *"Your Grief Will Turn to Joy."* This message was about the agony He went through! Why? He did it for us. He did it so that we may have peace, so that we may have Salvation. Are you going through difficulties? Do you feel your dream is fading and time is passing by? God shall surely bring to pass that dream. Trust God. He is preparing things for you. He is a faithful God. This mission work has been my dream even though the going was tough, I made up my mind to do just that.

Saturday 30th

Day 15

we visited Pastor Robert Kayanja's church in Kampala. I met him and spoke about the mission trip to both Uganda & Goma. He was very happy to see me. From there we went to Owino market in Kampala and other places then back to a sister called Maria - who was my host for two days.

Sunday March 31ˢᵗ

Day 16

My trip was now almost over. I still had two preaching appointments at two different churches. My first appointment was in Bunga (near lake victory) at Pastor Wilson's church. Then after that, we drove back to Faith Arena church at Kabowa on Entebbe road. I preached and many signs & wonders followed. Many souls were saved.

This had been an exciting and rewarding trip. The suffering, the long hours on the road, the sleepless nights in the jungles were all part of taking my cross and following Jesus. I could not have done it without Him.

My time in Uganda ended. My flight to Kenya departed from Entebbe at 8pm, Uganda time and landed safely at Jomo Kenyatta airport. My next flight took off at 9.40 pm, Kenya time –thank God. The time had come, and I boarded the plane home – to England. It was on this trip that the Lord spoke to me about church planting.

When I came back to London, I wanted to tell my husband, but knowing how he felt about church business, I could not sum up the courage to raise the subject. What

I did was ask God to direct me. The next day after I came back from the trip, to my surprise he called me from a tube station at Romford telling me about how the Lord had asked Him to start church planting.

Wow! God is good. He spoke to both of us about the notion of church planting and how we should go about it. The Lord gave us specific instructions on what to do. God is good.

Today God has blessed us with many churches around the world and many are yet to be planted. To God be the glory for all the things He has done.

Power Centre Church is a place for the hurting. We give solace and hope to people through prayers and the preaching of the undiluted Word of God. We also believe it is a place where old wounds can be healed, and our lives can be rebuilt through Jesus Christ.

Chapter 6
ETHIOPIAN MISSION EXPERIENCE

Sunday: 15.9.02

I am on my way to the airport. I checked in, and then later went into the departure lounge just in time for our flight to depart. We really had good service on board. Not much to say; as it was night and we all tried to sleep.

Monday: 16.9.02

We arrived at Addis Ababa Airport at 9am according to Ethiopian time.

My hosts were very nice, pleasant and God-fearing people. They picked me up from the airport. I was pleasantly surprised. They took me home; before I realised, it was almost bedtime. We prayed, sang and worshipped the Lord before we departed to our various rooms. However, before that, at the airport, the customs officers were searching everyone's baggage, but when it came to my turn, I could not even see anyone of them. Praise the Lord! I was told that because I was carrying so many gifts and some money, they could have charged me for bringing so many things into the country. God was in control. I passed through without any problem.

Tuesday: 17.9.02

We started planning for what we were going to do for the day. Mrs. Saba Gebru and I went to visit some places where they sell foodstuffs. We went to several places before we found what we wanted.

I was told it was better to speak to a lady who has been visiting those poor people's home with food etcetera. She came to the house where I was staying and explained things to me about how things are done in Ethiopia. We talked about places where the people are so poor; they live on the streets and eat garbage from the bin containers.

We spoke to some destitute families. Oh my God! It was so heart-breaking to see them in that condition. Some were sleeping on the concrete floor with just a piece of cloth on them. I was told some only had one meal in a day. I also visited an orphanage and spoke to the Director of the place. He told me how they have been helping the street children and also feeding them. I planned to visit them on Thursday.

Wednesday: 18.9.02

I was up about 6:30am, (Ethiopian time 1:30am) to get ready for our plans for the day. I had visited a place for the homeless to organise a meal for about 500 people or so for the day. I brought some tickets for some of them; these should bring them a free meal. We also brought some bags to put food in for the poor families, about 50 sets. Some families will get about 25-kilo bag of Teff, a local foodstuff which would last for about a month or more. Each family had about 5 to 10 people in the household.

We looked at prices of maize, tuff, sugar and other necessary things that could help them. The families we came across were mostly Christians but not all were Christians; we told them that even though we are a Christian organisation, we help everybody created by God.

My host was very happy about that; this is because two sets of families around them are not born again, charismatic Christians. Some were Ethiopian Orthodox, and some were non-Christians. We had a Bible study session that day at one of their friends' house. They invited me to share the Word of God and I gladly accepted.

Thursday: 19.9.02

This morning I woke up feeling the presence of the Lord around me. I was missing my family already, but still had a week and a half to go. It was now about 8am our time, but 5:00 pm Ethiopian time. I was told that that day, the 9th of September, according to the Ethiopia calendar, was 1995. And it's amazing. Their time difference was beyond my imagination; while it was about 1am it was about 7am. They have about three time zones in a day; 12 noon means 6:00pm. According to Mr. Tekka, Ethiopian's still uses the Old Testament timetable- so they have many things that are different from us.

Another interesting thing was when someone says to you, I will see you at 7:00 pm UK time it means 1:00pm Ethiopian time. I still could not fathom the calculation of different days and times. Their first week starts on Saturday and ends on Saturday. I was able to visit two families and gave them some of the donated items. Both families sent their blessings and greetings to all the partners who supported us.

They said, "May God bless and replace whatever you have given to feed the poor like us." Both thanked Jesus for using us to bless them with food to feed their children and grandmother.

God will bless us, she said, and this is the Word the man said in Psalm 28:6: *"Blessed be the Lord because He hath heard the voice of my supplications"*. He has sent you to help me and the Street Boys.

Friday: 20.9.02

On Friday morning, I was picked up by a street-preaching group to share the Word of God at their feeding time. The First group were about 20, 15 of them were between the ages of 14 – 21. I donated some bread and soup for their lunch. After that I preached the Word of God to them.

Not all these boys and men had a place to stay. They sleep on the street during the cold nights. The centre can only take a few people at a time and many more had to sleep rough in the streets. The only proper food they ate is during lunch; no breakfast and no supper. I was really touched when I saw a boy who was about 12 years old who was an orphan - no mother, no father or any relative; the street was the place he called home.

The second group was about 25—both youths and men. One man told me the story of his life. He was an owner of a fast-growing Ethiopian food restaurant in Sindam. He was making so much money, but later decided to go to Libya to look for proper living, hoping to start a business there; but he was arrested thinking he was a Jew coming to spy. He was imprisoned for about 8 years. Just as he was about to be released; he woke up one day and found himself in a hospital bed.

He later found out that one of his kidneys had been removed and given to someone else without his permission. Later on, he was released and deported to Ethiopia. He then found himself sleeping on the streets and begging for food.

Now by the grace of God the centre has taken him in for just a while until he finds somewhere to sleep and get money to start his own food business. He said the message I shared really blessed him. It has encouraged him to move forward and trust God for a new beginning.

At about 4pm, we went to the cemetery to bury one of my host's friends. She died and according to Ethiopian law, they had to bury her within six hours of her death. I had never seen anything like this; it was like being there during Jesus' time.

Everyone put on a white cloth over their head and were wailing like the time when Lazarus died. She died on the 20.9.02 according to the Ethiopian Calendar although the actual date was Sept 10, 1995.

Saturday: 21.9.02

At noon, we had just reached the centre where I paid and organised the feeding of poor families. I was surprised to see so many dirty people at the place including children. I preached a short message about Jesus feeding the five thousand people after the meal. During the altar call, I asked them if they wanted to give their lives to Jesus and get saved; almost all of them lifted their hands to receive Jesus. After that session, I helped them to serve the food. We fed over five hundred people and the Lord multiplied the food. The feeding centre reminded me of the story in the Bible when Jesus fed 5,000 men - (John 6:6-13).

You, our beloved partners paid for all the food. These people were so hungry; some had not eaten for days. Some walked from the border of Somalia to get there because of the conflicts in their country.

Some of these street boys, men, women and children including some babies born on the streets were there. After the meal, they thanked us for the food. I had a chat with a guy, who told me he was once a chief lorry driver in the district of Somalia and Ethiopia. As a result of the drought, he and his family had to move to Ethiopia to look for a job and the street is now his home, a home of hunger and despair.

He told me he was praying that God would cause someone to bless him with food today and as he was praying, he heard someone from England had come and had paid for food to be given to the street people. He took the chance and came. Thus, he thanked God for us feeding him. "May God bless our mission", he said.

After that we visited some homes; in fact, you could cry when you see where some women and their children were sleeping. Some of the places were so bad I did not have the heart to photograph them. I gave them some milk, soup, kerosene to cook their food and also gave them a local food called Teff, 25 kilos each. We visited about four (4) homes and donated essential items to them.

Sunday: 22.9.02

When it was time for church, I was given two choices as to where I would like to worship, either English African Church or Ethiopian Church. I chose the English service because of the language barrier I would encounter in the Ethiopian church. The service was not translated in English. The service was inspiring. There was a blend of different cultural groups there. The pastor called me to say a word or two to the people. I also met a diplomat from the Kenyan Embassy.

Later that day, we rested. I hoped that the following day I would have enough energy to continue with our mission.

My host took me to a local Ethiopian food restaurant where emperors used to have their meals when they chose to eat out. (Emperor Selassie).

Monday: 23.9.02

On Monday the 23.9.90, Ethiopian calendar 12.1.95, we went to visit 5 homes to give them Teff and other things. Giving things to people on the street can be very difficult because everyone wants some. I was told I could not control them and because people are needy, they will try to jump the queue and grab whatever they could lay their hands on.

The women were so grateful to the Lord for providing food for them. The food we gave them will last for at least a month or two. Already we had donated food to many families. They were all grateful; they believed that God had answered their cry by sending us to help them in their time of distress.

That year the rain failed to water the earth; so, most people were in danger of starvation. We still had more places to visit. These arrangements were better than giving to more people at the same time, as confusion may occur. The lady who worked with Compassion Charity advised me to share it wisely so that those in greater need would get their share.

I visited another man, who had been sick for some time and due to the financial problem had not been eating properly. On hearing this I gave him cornflakes and milk powder. In fact, the man did not know what to say to me. He was so happy because he could not eat anything else due to his illness; but when he tried the cornflakes with milk mixed with water, he really liked it. I left him some money to buy more oats so that he could have a proper breakfast. This would help him a lot for about 2 to 3 months at least until he can help himself.

Another place we went to made us realise how blessed we were. We visited an orphan's home. I was told that the mother died recently, and their 18-year-old sister had become their surrogate mother for the two other small children. I asked about their father. She told us that the last time they saw their father was when the last child was nine years old. Their story was very sad, and the older child had been trying to sell on the streets; the middle child, who was 12years old could not go to school because there was no one to pay the school fees; he had been selling paper hanky on the streets of Addis Ababa.

Another woman we visited was a former nun until she gave her life to Christ as her personal Saviour. Because of that, she was thrown out of the convent home and was now living in a horribly smelly place, where human beings should not be staying. She had nowhere else to go so she had to stay there and on top of it, she had no money to buy food. She was so grateful for the foodstuff I gave her. It would last her at least four months.

We donated food and clothing to a woman whose husband had been sick for about 6 months and had not been around; and due to his illness, he was unable to work and lost his job. They were about 9 people in a small house with one bedroom, which they shared with 7 children. I gave them some soup powder and showed, them how to mix it. This helped them because they did not know what they were going to eat that night. All they could say was "Thank you Lord for providing for us". We gave them 75 kg of Teff, packets of soup, plus other things that would last long. They did not even have money to buy kerosene, so we gave them some money to buy some. That day, we visited about 12 different families.

Tuesday: 24.9.02

At 6am Ethiopian time, we went to see a lady who had been sick for some time and had not been receiving proper medical attention. I was told a few years back she was going about selling things to feed her children as their father had passed away; but now she could not even feed herself, let alone feed her children. We donated 3/4 of a bag of Teff, which is a portion of food every Ethiopian eats. We also gave her some money to buy other things. In the afternoon, we visited an old lady who had been bedridden for some time without a family. She lived in a terrible place and on top of that, he had no supply of food. We gave her 5 packets of soup. I made one for her to show the person who had volunteered to prepare it for her how to do it. She was so glad that we came and donated some food to her since she had no one.

The Word of God in I John 3:17 says *"But whoso hath this world's good and seeth his brother or sister in need and shutteth up his bowels of compassionom him, how dwelleth the love of God in him?"*

Verse 18 says *"My little children,"* John Said, *"Let us not love in word, neither in tongue but in deed and truth."*

In the words "But if someone who is supposed to be a Christian has enough money to live well, and sees a brother in need, and won't help him- how can God's love be within him? Little children, let us stop just saying we love people; let us really love them and show it by our actions. Then we will know for sure, by our actions, that we are on God's side, and our consciences will be clear, even when we stand before the Lord".

The donations of our friends and partners made it possible for us to assist many poor and destitute families; some came from the war zone, some were orphans, widows, and children. Some lived in appalling situations, street children without homes; some had not had a bath for two months, because there was no place for them.

Even though we could not solve all their problems for them, we helped to make their lives a little better.

Some of the families we visited could now eat for a long time because we did not just feed them for a day, but we provided food for them that will last for about 5 months or more. Even some of the money we gave them to trade with will last for a long time – this will enable them to provide for themselves and their families. £20 is enough capital for a lady to trade and feed her children.

Wednesday 25.9.02

Just imagine you are watching a video of this lady who came from Eritrea and due to the fighting over there faced many difficult situations. I was introduced to this woman by one of the ladies who had been helping me to visit the destitute families. She told me, she overheard someone say that there is a woman from England who had been helping the poor; so, she brought her case to us. In fact, when I visited her house I almost vomited. She lived in a place where animals in the west will never be put; it would be cruel to put dogs in that house let alone a human being.

This poor and destitute woman was given this room to live in as a favour from someone; the roof was leaking so much that when it rains the children cover themselves with plastic bags in a room. "It felt like sleeping on the roadside", she told me.

On seeing the situation, I asked how we could be of help to her. Her only solution was for us to help fix the roof so that the children could have a good sleep away from mosquitoes and rain. In fact, with just £50 this problem was solved. I wanted to cry while I was in the house. I also noticed the place where the children were sleeping with their mum; I wish you could see the video for yourself. She also told me she had been trying to survive day by day by the Grace of God; she didn't even know what she and the children were going to eat that day.

The rain was threatening to fall, and she just wanted to thank God for everyone that gave money to me to come and be a blessing to them. She would be forever grateful to God and us for the wonderful gifts we gave them. She repeatedly said, "God bless them who gave for you to come and be of help to us." I also blessed her with some money to buy her sons some school uniform, kerosene and also to pay for their school fees.

This reminds me of what 2 Corinthians 9: 6-15 says. When Paul wrote to the Corinthians, he said in verse 11 that, *"He that soweth sparingly shall reap also sparingly; and he which soweth bountifully shall reap also bountifully...".* When we delivered the gifts to those who are in need, they pray for you and asked God to richly bless you. Two good things happen because of the gifts - Those in need were helped, and they rejoiced and gave thanks to God. The people we helped were eternally grateful for the generous gifts and praised God for His grace, loving-kindness and faithfulness. Also, they prayed for all our donors with deep fervour for graciously helping them.

Some of us may feel that we do not have much to offer people in need. You may not have much to give but whatever you give goes a long way in promoting and spreading the gospel of Jesus Christ to the nations. May I implore you to continue to support Wood World Missions in our propagation of the gospel and with our assisting of people in dire need of help. God will richly bless you all for your donations and offerings. What you may consider a meagre gift might be what changes people's lives and saves them.

The Bible tells us in Hebrews 13:16 that *"But to do good and to communicate forget not: for with such sacrifice God is well-pleased. Also, in psalm 112:9 God says to us "He hath disperse, he hath given to the poor; his righteousness endureth forever, His horn shall be exalted with honour".*

Almost everyone that was touched by our donation had one thing in common: They praised God for deliverance and mercy. They thanked God for your lives. It also increased their love for the Lord and increased their faith in God. They were eager and open to receive the Word of God because of the love we showed them by our giving.

They were full of joy and thanksgiving when we blessed them with the food, clothing and finance. Their faces lit up, the children were laughing, playing and thanking God. The joy of seeing their delight and jubilation was elating and heart-warming. Thanks be to God for his mercies that endureth forever. This trip was not man-made. I tell you. It was God's plan for us to help the destitute people; even if it was for a brief period.

What inspired me to go to these needy people? It was the love of Christ inside me. I was touched by people dying without making Jesus the Lord and Saviour of their lives. I wanted to bring the gospel to people who had not heard about Jesus and to encourage them to re-dedicate their lives to Jesus. Some people had only witnessed violence such as shootings, killings and suffering. The good news had to be preached to them. My aim in going to these places was to bring hope and the gospel to these people.

Thursday: 26.9.02

My mission trip was very fruitful and beneficial. Many poor families were blessed, helped and encouraged with the Word of God. Some people received their breakthroughs in diverse ways – glory to God. I had the opportunity to organise prayer meetings in which people were blessed.

People testified of the goodness of God and some people received healing from chronic illnesses. May Jesus be glorified.

God bless you all.

Chapter 7
WHAT INSPIRES ME TO DO WHAT I DO?

I am an Evangelist called by God and I believe that God will guide and give me the strength and foresight to do His work. I was called by God to go and be a witness for Him. He has commissioned me to spread the gospel and I am determined to do His will.

Since I was a little girl, I have desired to see people happy and to make a difference. I am sure you will help me make this childhood dream come true. My greatest wish is to motivate and teach these people to be self-reliant and to enable them to grow crops and feed themselves, even at a subsistence level. We hope to provide them with tools and to empower them to fend for themselves and guide them to become independent. I am sure this is achievable by the grace of God. This vision should go together with the spreading of the gospel and getting people to have a personal relationship with God. Christ came to this world to demonstrate love for his people and to save sinners. He came to give freedom to all. He came to give liberty, autonomy, choice, freewill and sovereignty to all. He loves us and wants His children to prosper.

My Inspiration About Touching Lives

My inspiration means:

- Seek—is to seek souls for Christ
- Aim—is to do the Will of God
- Hope—Hoping for the best from God
- Desire—is to desire only to please Him
- Want—is to see people's life transformed for the better and to the glory of God
- Wish—is to fulfil my missionary-calling

If you have all these qualities, then God has called you into missionary work. Missionary work is not bread and butter, it is hard work. You have to be called by God, otherwise you will not be able to do it. God is calling all of us into his service, let's respond to him.

God is awesome, faithfully and he answers prayers. My aspiration is to repair the dilapidated houses for these women and their children whom I spoke about earlier.

Jesus came to set the captives free. He came to save the poor, the penniless, the impoverished, the insolvent and the needy. That is why Apostle Paul encouraged the Corinthians to give gifts to the needy. The receivers will welcome the gifts and will break out in songs and thanksgiving. They will praise God and rejoice—2 Corinthians 9:9-15.

Wood World Missions sponsored about four of them by putting roofs over their heads, by training them and by empowering them to look forward to the future with hope.

Saturday: 28.9.02

We checked the flights, then after that, I was taken to the Ghana High Commissioner's residence. We later went with the high commissioner and his family to the Ghanaian fellowship association. I was warmly welcomed, and I too was happy to meet Ghanaians over there because for almost two weeks in Ethiopia, I had not met any Ghanaians. It was nice to meet them. What a day! I thank God Almighty.

I have decided to narrate these case studies so that you can get a clear picture of why we need to go to these places, feed the people and share the love of Christ. God wants us to help the less fortunate. We should always think about the less fortunate and strive to help them as God commanded us to do.

Despite the evil in this world, we must make every effort to bring a ray of sunshine into the lives of our destitute and oppressed fellow human beings. We must not be satisfied with our comfort; we must try to help less fortunate people by being charitable towards them. Paul says that we should try to influence or win men and women everywhere, endeavour to see them change their minds about following Christ. (2 Corinthians 5:11).

Jesus Christ, our example said in Luke 4:18 that *"The Spirit of the Lord is upon me because he hath anointed me to preach the gospel to the poor; he hath sent me to heal the broken-hearted, to preach deliverance to the captives, and recovering of sight to the blind, to set at liberty them that are bruised ".*

Isaiah 61:1-3 also says:- *"The Spirit of the Lord GOD is upon me; because the LORD hath anointed me to preach good tidings unto the meek; he hath sent me to bind up the brokenhearted, to proclaim liberty to the captives, and the opening of the prison to them that are bound; To proclaim the acceptable year of the LORD, and the day of vengeance of our God; to comfort all that mourn;*

To appoint unto them that mourn in Zion, to give unto them beauty for ashes, the oil of joy for mourning, the garment of praise for the spirit of heaviness; that they might be called trees of righteousness, the planting of the LORD, that he might be glorified".

Our Lord Jesus came to this earth with a *Mission*. And when He was about to go He re-assigned it to us in Matthews 28:18-20:- *"And Jesus came and spake unto them, saying, All power is given unto me in heaven and in earth. Go ye therefore, and teach all nations, baptizing them in the name of the Father, and of the Son, and of the Holy Ghost: Teaching them to observe all things whatsoever I have commanded you: and, lo, I am with you always, even unto the end of the world".*

Jesus is the Messiah who is saying to us to go and help these destitute people; if we do so, He will be with us even until the end.

The Love of God compels me to do what I do because it was love that took Jesus to the Cross. This selfless love really touched my heart and I hope it would also actively encourage you to support our mission work.

We should not rely on man, but we must rely on Jesus for guidance and direction. We must be determined to do the will of the Father; we must encourage the lost souls into the Kingdom. We are ambassadors of Christ. We must take up this challenge by spreading the gospel and helping the less fortunate people to live better lives in Christ. We must reach the needy with the Word of God. Jesus will help you and I by touching the heart of people to support and provide material and spiritual provision to help those in need.

Do you know your mission call? Let us look at a few definitions of our Mission call:

What Is a Mission Call?

Mission—means:

1) Assignment
2) Task
3) Job
4) Projects
5) Duty / Obligation
6) Chore
7) Commission

We are Ambassadors of Christ: Matthew 28:18-20.

Mission also means:

a. Sending a person or a number of people on some special work
b. A particular task or goal assigned to a person or group
c. A body of people sent to propagate religious faith

A missionary is a person sent to another country to tell people about Christ. Are you available to be used? You do not need to travel; you can be used right here in the United Kingdom.

An *Ambassador* is a person sent to another country to look after the affairs of the government and, in our case, to represent Christ and His Kingdom. We all have an obligation to witness to people and to share the love of Jesus with them. We have been called to bear witness on behalf of God. For instance, Apostle Paul was a brilliant spokesperson for Christ. We all may not have the confidence to go around the world preaching the gospel, but we can start from our Jerusalem and then to the outermost parts of the world.

When we travelled to Athens in 1993, I remember visiting the area in Athens where Apostle Paul preached the Gospel in Acts 17:16-34. It felt good just being there. You may sometimes feel discouraged because you do not get support about what you really want to do for God. We all go through hard times especially as we try to pursue our calling, but if God has called you to go on mission trips, you must obey His instruction. He will assist you. Trusting God is the best thing to do. We all have a mission call. Jesus had a mission, too.

In Isaiah 48:15, the scripture describes Jesus' mission statement by confirming the prophetic word God showed him about Jesus: *"I, even I, have spoken; yea, I have called him: I have brought him, and he shall make his way prosperous,"* meaning Jesus will succeed in His earthly missionary work.

When Jesus came to the earth, He saw the poor people. Isaiah was prophesying about this long before Jesus came. We all know from experience the depths of suffering, affliction, let-downs, and brokenness caused by the people we love. We know the pain we went through. Jesus knows all. That is why He came. After He left this earth, He gave us the commission to witness to those who may be facing similar situations.

God showed mercy to the merciless and salvation to mankind who do not even deserve it. Will you show mercy to others? Will you go out to the communities of the world and show people the love of Christ? While we were yet sinners and horrible, terrible, nasty, atrocious, hideous in the sight of God, He helped us, cleansed us from evil with the blood of His own beloved Son Jesus Christ. He has now adopted us into his own family, lavishing us with many blessings.

Jesus is asking you to help in spreading the Gospel. Rise to the challenge and God will richly bless you.

Eyewitness!

The things I witness on my mission trips are usually emotional and disheartening. It is never easy to witness destitute, unfortunate, and deprived young boys, girls, mothers, and fathers scavenging rubbish bins in order to eat. No human being should suffer in that manner. We have made a pledge to help feed these street youths. At least they would have a nice warm meal. Your help will always be appreciated.

We will also continue to make more inquiries to see what we can do to help some of them learn new skills. This would equip them to provide for themselves and their families and this would enhance their self-respect and reduce their dependability on handouts.

We visited and spoke to some very poor and desperate families who did not know where the next meal was coming from. The mother told us how she was praying to God for help and lo and behold we knocked on their door and offered them some soup and milk powder. We also bought her 75 kilos of Teff (a local Ethiopian food) that would last for about two or three months. We also gave her some money to buy kerosene for the lamp as well as for cooking. We gave her some money to trade with in order to help the rest of the family. This woman's husband used to work as a guard, but he fell ill and could no longer work. As a result, he could not feed his seven children, himself and his wife. They were very happy to receive our donation. They praised God for answering their cry.

We visited a centre called HOPE where we met people fleeing from the war zone. They were at the centre hoping to get leftovers. They were also begging for food and money. We arranged with the director of the centre to provide food for about 500 people. The people were overjoyed and thanked us. I told them that God spoke to one of our members called Rev. Chris Tubridy, who bought my plane ticket to come and be a blessing to them. The people saw that there is always hope if you trust in God. God multiplied the food. Everybody got something to eat and there were a lot of leftovers. God is a good God.

The sick man who told us that he had not been eating was overjoyed. He did not even know what to do with himself. He thanked us for coming to be a blessing to him and his wife who had been begging in the streets to provide food for both of them. He was 75 years old. These are his words in Psalm 28:6 - *"Blessed be the LORD, because He hath heard the voice of my supplications. He is my strength, my shield from every danger. I trusted in Him, and He helped me. Joy rises in my heart until I burst out into songs of praise to Him. The Lord protects His people and gives victory to his anointed king. Defend your people, Lord; defend and bless your chosen ones. Lead them like a shepherd and carry them forever in your arms. He has sent you to help me in my need".*

Within the next two days we visited him again only to find him standing outside his home. Incredible; poverty is a terrible disease. We thank God for saving him.

We gave essential items to many families who were desperate and destitute. One woman and her children were so poor to the point where they believed there was no hope for them. In fact, if God did not intervene in their situation, I believe eventually one of them would have died with pneumonia because the place where they were sleeping was so smelly, filthy and terrible. The roof of the building was leaking so badly that when it rained in the night the children had to cover themselves with plastic. The water comes straight into the room. By God's grace, we changed the old roof and put new roofing sheets on. We bought her a stove and gave her some money to buy kerosene so that she could prepare the children some hot meals to eat. We gave her 3 blankets and they were grateful for the gifts.

I have so many things to say. How can we repay the Lord for all his goodness? Our answer should be: *"I will lift up the cup of salvation and call on the name of the Lord". — Psalm 116:12.*

Our mission for the world is simple. We are grateful to Jesus for making it possible for us to help people who are less fortunate than us and to spread the gospel. Jesus is our Lord and master. We try to go one step beyond local evangelism to lift up God's cup of salvation so that men, women, boys and girls can drink of the same life-giving water. The Bible says that we are to witness in Jerusalem (where we are) in Judea and Samaria (which are the regions nearby) and unto the ends of the earth (the World).

Today is the best day to witness for Christ. Tomorrow will never come if we do not witness today. Tomorrow is always tomorrow it never comes. However, today always comes because today is today. Get ready and do something for God.

If you cannot go far into the world, you can do something by witnessing locally. You can give to those missionaries who travel to places to tell the story of our Lord and saviour Jesus Christ.

Someone needs to tell them about:

1) the fear of God
2) Our need for God
3) God's love
4) the reality of eternity
5) the great testimonies we have to tell

We should also give our best to support mission work, locally and abroad.

The Bible tells us about the importance of making every man, woman, boy and girl hear the gospel; the message that reunites man with God. The great commission in Mark 16: 14-16 should encourage us to do just that; this is because each one of us have valuable testimonies to give and to tell. We can even testify about how we were saved. Jesus left us this vital task. We all should go into the world and preach the Gospel to the broken hearted, the poor and cast out demons. We can do this with the power of God. Without Him we can do nothing. With God, everything is possible.

What is the Gospel we preach?

It is the power of God available to believers. In Romans 1.16, Paul tells us that Christ, God's Son died for our sins; He was buried and that He was raised on the third day according to the scriptures. (1 Corinthians 15:1-4).

We must believe that God exists and that he is a rewarder of all who diligently seek him. He is not a malicious, distant old man sitting somewhere who does not care about us. (Hebrews 11:6)

We must believe that He is a Holy God and that our many sins of not seeking him, of going our own way, of our many bad thoughts, words and actions have separated us from His love and presence. As a result, if we do not repent before we die, we can only expect punishment. God said in Roman 3:22 that He will accept and acquit us—declare us not guilty if we trust Jesus Christ to take away our sins. And we all can be saved in this same way, by coming to Christ, no matter who we are or what we have been like or done. Apostle Paul continues in verse 23 saying, *"Indeed we all have sinned; and have all fallen short of God's glorious plan; yet now He*

God himself declares us not guilty of offending Him if we trust Jesus Christ who in His kindness freely takes away our sins".

Roman 6:23. Says, *"For the wages of sin is death, but the free gift of God is eternal life through Jesus Christ our Lord"*

God in his great love sent his Son Jesus, born of a virgin and sinless, to rescue us by taking all of God's righteous anger so that we might have peace and be able to enter God's Holy presence both now and at death. (1 Peter 2:24-25).

It is our duty as Christians to act and behave according to the teachings of the Bible so that we would have eternal life. We must confess and genuinely feel sorry for our sins. We must believe that Jesus died because of us and we must ask him to forgive our sins. We must make Jesus the Lord and Saviour of our lives. *"God so loved the world, that he gave his one and only Son, that whoever believes in him should not perish, but have eternal life"* – John 3:16. We must cherish this gift and ask Jesus to come into our hearts and ask him to be Lord and Saviour our lives.

Revelation 3.20 tells us that Jesus is standing and knocking at our door. We must acknowledge him, open the door to our hearts and ask him to come in and live in us. Would you witness to people and encourage them to accept Jesus as their Lord and Saviour? He is waiting for your invitation. He will surely bless you.

Today is always the day to receive God's salvation, and now is always the best time because tomorrow may be too late. For these reasons, we who believe should stand firm, not allowing anything to move us from these eternal truths. We should always give ourselves fully to the work of the Lord, telling others, knowing that our labour will not go in vain or fall on deaf ears—1 Corinthians 15:58

If it is God's will, for us to witness, be ready to face the challenges. Do whatever you can, and God will back you up. Some people will not listen to you. Even if they laugh at you scornfully, do not give up, persevere and God will richly bless you.

When I was called, some people did not believe me. Some of them said how could God call her. Is she not the girl next door; did we not use to sit and drink alcohol with her? My fellow brethren, if you have been in that situation before, you are not alone. God will strengthen and direct you. Jesus died for us all and he wants all of us to be saved.

Mark 1:45 says that people came to Jesus from everywhere. They came to Jesus because they needed a Saviour or perhaps because they wanted resolutions to their problems or because of the testimonies that people recounted. This reminds me of a lady I met on one of my mission trips. She was jubilant and wanted everyone to know that Jesus had touched her. Let us tell people about Jesus by telling them about our testimonies – about what He has done for us. I love my missionary work. I do not think I can do anything else; it gives me joy and fulfilment in God.

Some people say, '*Why should I evangelise? That is not my calling.*' As believers in Christ, we have been called to bear witness. Evangelism is at the core of what God is doing today. God has a job for us on this earth.

When Jesus came, He too gave us the commission to go out, preach the gospel, and win souls for the Kingdom. Jesus has called you to be a witness. He is saying *"You did not choose me; I chose you to win souls and to teach them about the goodness of God. I am the Way, the Truth and the life and if you obey my calling, I the Lord will guide and prosper you."*

Do you hunger for God? Do you hunger for those poor soul's that are perishing? When Jesus came to this earth, He had a mission; He had a purpose. His messages were always very simple and clear: *"Repent, for the kingdom of God has come near,"* and "*I came to seek and to save the lost*". Jesus desires that we should all witness and win souls.

One thing I have discovered in churches is that when you encourage people to witness, only a few people come forward—the same faces all the time. But yet in the church, those who don't come at all are the ones who complain. They are the ones who say "we are not growing, how come? Yet, when you call them for evangelism, they always have somewhere to go. The lost souls should motivate us to evangelise.

The love of God should motivate us. Although many are called, few are chosen; we must still strive to go out and win souls for Christ. Some are called to go on mission trips, but others can make an impact locally. Some are called to assist financially in ministry. Some are called to prayer for Missionaries. People are not always willing to take up the challenge to serve God. They prefer to take back seats. Jesus wants us to do what He did when He was on this earth.

The church is made up of those who are enlightened in the word of God, have tasted the heavenly gifts, and sampled the goodness of the Word of God. The churches of Christ also made up of sinners entering for the first time and those who have already been saved.

However, we can all be used to evangelise to different people of the world. Some of us are outgoing and could go where others cannot go; others may be shy but still there is always a way those shy people can witness. For example, dropping leaflets in homes. With leaflet distribution, you do not need to talk to people.

Jesus evangelised with love and gave salvation to people. You too can show love by sharing the word of God with people and inviting them into the fellowship of Christians. You are the church; did you know that? The building in which we meet every Sunday is just a building. You are the church.

People see you when you witness to them. Jesus lives inside us. That is why He said, *"Let your light so shine so that people will see Jesus in you".* Our attitude should reflect Jesus, and this should draw people into the fellowship.

How Can One Become a Witness for Jesus?

Let us begin with you, the individual member. It is true that as an individual you can be very effective in your daily life. If you live out your faith, speak naturally of your love for the Lord and for your church, people will have respect for you, and they will take you seriously. When you invite someone who does not go to church to come to church with you, or to come to a special programme with you, they will come with you and in so doing you are not only bringing that brother or sister into the church, but you are doing the work of a witness. We as the church should encourage each other to take up the challenge; go out and be a witness for Christ and his kingdom.

Apart from sharing the Word of God with the unsaved, we must also invite them to Church so that they too can have a home church in order to grow in Christ.

Another powerful thing we can do is to encourage each other in our daily witnessing exercise.

Jesus Christ is the Good News and He is the same yesterday, today, and forever. His word is still the same today. Your crown is waiting for you.

Chapter 8
MALAWI MISSION EXPERIENCE

Wood World Missions in Malawi

I received an alarming email from a pastor in Malawi regarding the appalling state of the orphans. In addition, he sent me disturbing and graphic pictures of the suffering that was going on in Malawi. In fact, that was the first time I heard about Malawi, even though I have travelled around the continent of Africa. Malawi never crossed my mind before then. He begged us to come, preach, and help his churches, as he believed the Lord wanted him to let us plant churches in Malawi. We explained to him that we did not want to come to start churches, but to be a blessing to the poor and that it was for him and his leaders to run the churches. He protested. He gave a testimony that he and his people knew that they were to work under the headship of our ministry.

After much prayer, we decided to go and help. The day came when I arrived at the airport in Blantyne. I was taken to their home, which is what I requested so that I could donate the hotel money to support them.

The next day we went out to visit the sick, those with Aids and HIV. We bought food, clothes and other necessary things for them. I was taken to the church with many orphans who were waiting for their supplies of maize, sugar and the dried fish that we had brought to donate to them.

I later found out that they were not based in one place but came from individual homes and other churches but that did not matter to me as some had lost both parents. The next day we went from house to house visiting the sick and also donating food items to them. We also held crusades in different marketplaces and set up churches where there was no church. We re-started some churches which were closed down due to lack of funding. Many people gave their lives to Christ as they saw we were not only preaching the word of God, but we were also providing them with material help as well.

For the next few days we went from the South of Malawi to the North preaching the gospel of Christ as well as providing essential items for the people in need.

We set up many churches and adopted others along the way. Brothers and Sister let me warn you about this; not everyone claiming to be a pastor is indeed a Pastor. I found out the hard way. Because of poverty, people would lie to you in order to acquire things from you for themselves. People would tell stories to evoke sympathy from you and to get something from you.

Then they would move on to someone they deem as an easier prey. Be warned as I have seen and learnt on my missionary journeys; when you adopt a church in any country, make sure you do your homework, otherwise, you will be betrayed and abandoned when they find out that you do not have lots of money to dish out to them.

The pastor deceived me and left me dumbfounded. I remember how I felt when he told me how he lost his churches because he had no money and that someone took over the churches. Everything was going on well, until I brought a friend from the USA to join me there.

As soon as I turned my back, the story changed. I loved this man and his family dearly, but I needed to use this experience to warn others. When my friend told me about his deceit, I was very furious at first, but I forgave him and took him back again as our coordinator.

After that I took another friend from the UK along with me to Malawi. Everything was going on well, I thought, until one of the guys warned me about what my then coordinator was planning to do. I was betrayed. Mercy, what is wrong with you, I asked myself.

My heart sank when I heard of his plans, because he had seen the white friends of mine, he thought GOLD had landed. He thought the white people I brought were my bosses. He said to himself, "If these people are supporting Mercy, then I will do anything for them to support me directly rather than through Mercy." He was wrong. The white woman was not my boss.

I was contemplating not going back to Malawi, but then, that night the Lord began to melt my heart after I received several letters and words from the paramount chief not to give up. I went back. But I decided never to work with him again. I had forgiven him, but I decided not to work with him ever again. This is what one of the local pastors emailed me:

Dear Pastor Mercy Wood,

"I heard what happened to you again in Malawi. Please do not stop what you are doing here, as these children need the support of your ministry."

May God teach that pastor to be honest. I plead with you to forgive him. Let God alone judge him. I pray that God would enable you to come across the right people. I will not like to see what happened in the past happen again. As an Overseer for more than 18 years, I have come across so many pastors who have cheated me; and I know how it hurts to be deceived. I know, not many people serve the Lord with a sincere heart. They serve the Lord to satisfy their evil desires and their bellies. What they say is not what happens. May God help us to be honest in all our dealings. May the truth set us free. May God help us to be honest in our dealings with others. The truth sets us free. May God help me to be honest in Jesus' name.

Pastor Howard Ngwira (Malawi North)

Even though I had forgiven him, for 7 years he was still pleading and asking for forgiveness; I had forgiven him but was never going to work with him again. We still talk when I go to Malawi. When he is in need, I try my best to help him; but I could not take the chance to trust him and work with him a third time.

Today, our friend, Pastor Randy McEwen from Acts 3 Ministries in the USA is doing wonderful work in the South of Malawi. Today Acts 3 Ministries has a school and a branch church in Nderendi. We kept our relationship with him.

Our Ministry (Wood World Missions and Power Centre Church) also has a school in the South of Malawi which is also used as a Church and a Community hall. Thanks to Elder Neema Ndovie who is our coordinator in the South of Malawi. All glory be to our God.

We are more than conquerors according to Romans 8:37— *"Nay, in all these things we are more than conquerors through him that loved us".*

You are a victor and a conqueror. In Christ we are:

- Victorious – Winning
- Triumphant- Glorious
- Champions – Winner
- Successful- Unbeatable

Today, we have 8 orphan centres and over 35 PCC branches in Malawi. We also have the privilege of providing free Christian materials to pastors, preaching in hospitals, orphanages homes and ministries in the villages.

The Churches have many needs: They need Bibles, Tracts, Musical Instruments, Film Projectors, Megaphones, Generators and other such needs in order to expand the work of God.

We do a lot of good works and charitable deeds in Nigeria, too. We currently have a Power Centre Church branch in Lagos, Nigeria. We are also fully registered as a Charity in Nigeria. Glory be to God.

In relation to Ghana, we have been doing charity and missionary work in Ghana since 1994 up till date. By the grace of God, we now have 26 PCC branch Churches all across Ghana.

In Ghana, we currently have Two schools – From Nursery to JHS - one in Akosombo and the other in Koforidua, Asokore. We are currently building a Secondary Technical Vocational School in Akosombo. We are being helped by the New African Nation. We are also building a Hostel in Adjena in Ghana for the youth in that township. This has been a 10-year vision now coming to pass.

As for my full Missionary experiences in Ghana and Nigeria, I will leave it for now till my next book.

Please help us *Financially*, *Materially* and in *Prayers*. Please you can donate whatever God directs you to give.

2 Corinthians 9:6-15 says: *"But this I say, He which soweth sparingly shall reap also sparingly; and he which soweth bountifully shall reap also bountifully. Every man according as he purposeth in his heart, so let him give; not*

grudgingly, or of necessity: for God loveth a cheerful giver. And God is able to make all grace abound toward you; that ye, always having all sufficiency in all things, may abound to every good work: (As it is written, He hath dispersed abroad; he hath given to the poor: his righteousness remaineth for ever. Now he that ministereth seed to the sower both minister bread for your food, and multiply your seed sown, and increase the fruits of your righteousness;) Being enriched in every thing to all bountifulness, which causeth through us thanksgiving to God. For the administration of this service not only supplieth the want of the saints, but is abundant also by many thanksgivings unto God; Whiles by the experiment of this ministration they glorify God for your professed subjection unto the gospel of Christ, and for your liberal distribution unto them, and unto all men; And by their prayer for you, which long after you for the exceeding grace of God in you. Thanks be unto God for his unspeakable gift."

HOLDING SICK PEOPLE

I have held in my arms dying people suffering from AIDS through no fault of theirs. The majority of them are tainted with abusive and traumatic experiences. I have felt the tears of innocent orphans dying of hunger on my shoulder and seen the miraculous transformation in their faces - only Christ can bring this to them through us. I have watched men, women and orphans receive desperately needed food and other basic essentials.

By donating to *Wood World Missions Appeal*, you will be helping to accomplish the following:

a) Given a widow who is ready to commit suicide food to feed her hungry children.
b) Providing a poverty-stricken family with decent clothing and shoes.
c) Helping the youth to learn a trade, acquire skills to support themselves and their communities.

d) Giving an out of work father enough food and money to feed his family.
e) Most of all you will have sent a life-changing message of the Gospel to the people of Malawi and around the world.

The Bible says in Mathew 25:35 that, *"For I was an hungred, and ye gave me meat: I was thirsty, and ye gave me drink: I was a stranger, and ye took me in."*

Any amount you donate will be greatly appreciated. May the good Lord richly bless you and give you a hundred-fold Harvest.

WOOD WORLD MISSIONS PRAYER PARTNERS

Becoming a prayer partner with Wood World Missions.

Prayer Targets:

1. Wisdom in planning meetings.
2. Breakthroughs.
3. Doors of opportunities,
4. Financial blessing to meet the needs of the mission's projects. Increase prayer & Financial support for the Missions.
5. Harvest of souls and healing.
6. Success in our Prison ministries.
7. Increase of God's anointing over every Minister and partner of Wood World Missions.

We believe that God answers prayers; so please continue to pray for WWM and PCC.
If you are interested in becoming a partner for life with WWM, please:
Email us: woodworldmissions@hotmail.com
Call our mission office on: 020 8286 3018
My mobile number: +233 (0) 264 756 653.
You can also visit our website and go to the supporters' site and fill the form there. www.pccwwm.org

WOOD WORLD MISSIONS FINANCIAL PARTNERS

Becoming a financial supporter of the

Wood World Missions

Please tick the following boxes appropriate to your response:

I would like to make a personal donation to the work of Wood World Missions.

- ○ I enclose a gift of £........ one-off or £.............every month.
- ○ would like information about making donations by standing order.
- ○ I would like to leave a legacy gift to the charity work of the Wood World Missions.
- ○ I would like to make a regular monthly / quarterly donation of £5, £10, £15 £20, £25, £50 or other.... to the WWM.

   Amount in Words:..........................

Personal Details:

- ○ I would like the WWM to claim the amount I have given under the Gift Aid scheme.
- ○ I am a UK Taxpayer.

All Cheques to be made payable to Wood World Missions

TITLE: (Revd., Dr, Mr., Mrs., Miss, Ms.,)

Name..

Address..

Post Code..

Country..

Signature:........................... Date:......................................

Or you can donate

Via: www.paypal.com
Using:"mailto:anydonation@woodworldmissions.org"
anydonation@woodworldmissions.org
or "mailto:revdrwood@aol.co.uk"
revdrwood@aol.co.uk

You can also donate direct. Visit our charity website:
http://www.pccwwm.org or www.pccwwm.org

Address:

Bishop Dr Mercy Wood:
+44 (0) 7719411672
+44 (0) 7425360466
+233 (0) 264756653
Email: woodworldmissions@hotmail.com
woodworldmissions@hotmail.com
UK Address:
238-240 London Road,
Mitcham, Surrey,
CR4 3HD United Kingdom

Jesus said the harvest is plenteous, but the labourers are few. We should be inspired and motivated to go out and witness for Christ.

God bless you.

Printed in Great Britain
by Amazon